# FIRST GUITAR SCALES

**Wise Publications**
London/New York/Paris/Sydney/Copenhagen/Madrid

**Exclusive Distributors:**
*Music Sales Limited*
**8/9 Frith Street,**
**London W1V 5TZ, England.**
*Music Sales Pty Limited*
**120 Rothschild Avenue,**
**Rosebery, NSW 2018,**
**Australia.**

**Order No.AM91074**
**ISBN 0.7119.3405.3**
**This book © Copyright 1993 by Wise Publications**

*Cover design by Pearce Marchbank, Studio Twenty*
*Cover photography by George Taylor*
*Compiled and arranged by Andy Jones*
*Computer management by Adam Hay Editorial Design*
*Music processed by The Pitts*

*Your Guarantee of Quality*
**As publishers, we strive to produce every book to**
**the highest commercial standards.**
**Particular care has been given to specifying acid-free,**
**neutral-sized paper which has not been chlorine bleached but**
**produced with special regard for the environment. Throughout,**
**the printing and binding have been planned to ensure a sturdy,**
**attractive publication which should give years of enjoyment.**
**If your copy fails to meet our high standards,**
**please inform us and we will gladly replace it.**

**Music Sales' complete catalogue lists thousands of titles**
**and is free from your local music shop,**
**or direct from Music Sales Limited.**
**Please send a cheque/postal order for £1.50 for postage to:**
**Music Sales Limited, Newmarket Road,**
**Bury St. Edmunds, Suffolk IP33 3YB.**

In this book we will use both standard musical notation (used by all instrumentalists) and guitar tablature (a simplified diagram-style system peculiar to the guitar).

Standard music notation uses a set of 5 lines, called the stave or staff. Note symbols are placed on lines and the spaces between the lines to denote the various musical sounds.

Lines:   Spaces:

We can also extend the range of the notation above and below the stave's 5 lines:

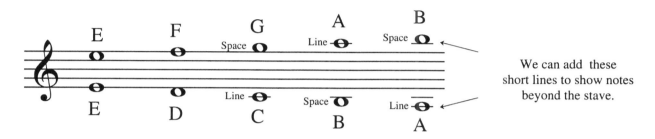

We can add these
short lines to show notes
beyond the stave.

If the symbol ♯ is placed in front of a note in a piece of music, the note found next to the sign is sharpened (raised one fret).
If the symbol ♭ is placed in front of a note in a piece of music, the note found next to the sign is flattened (lowered by one fret).

The symbol ♮ cancels the previous ♯ or ♭.

If a sharp ♯ or flat ♭ sign is placed at the beginning of a stave in front of the time signature, it means that all the notes in the piece that occur on this line or anywhere on the stave are affected.

Tablature is a map of the fretboard showing the 6 strings of the guitar. The top line in the diagram corresponds to the top string of the guitar – the one nearest your feet when you play.

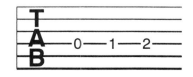

The numbers on the stave show which fret to finger.
0 = open string, 1 = 1st fret, 2 = 2nd fret etc.

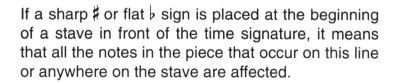

Music is comprised of sounds of different lengths. We have a simple system for describing the duration of musical notes:

| Whole Note | Half Note | Quarter Note |
|:---:|:---:|:---:|
| 4 beats long | 2 beats long | 1 beat long |

The two numbers at the start of this example are the 'time signature'.
Here this means the music is divided into units equal to 4 quarter notes (units of four beats each).

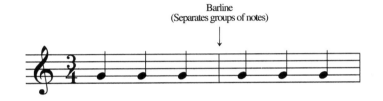

In this example the music is grouped into units of 3 beats each.

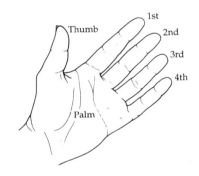

Fretting Hand: Palm Up
(Left hand for right-handed players).

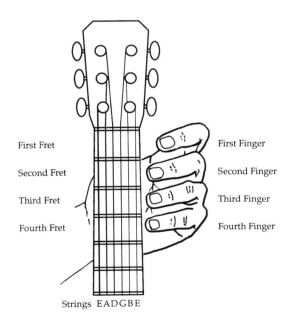

When starting on the guitar it is best to use one finger to one fret where possible:
Here the first finger covers the 1st fret space (between the nut and the 1st brass fret).
The second finger covers the 2nd fret.
The third finger covers the 3rd fret.
The fourth finger covers the 4th fret.

Accurate tuning of the guitar is essential. If the guitar is out of tune, the scale structure will sound incorrect and the end result will not help with the learning process.
The guitar can be tuned with the aid of pitch pipes or dedicated electronic guitar tuners which are available through your local music dealer.

If you do not have a tuning device, tuning can be achieved by a process called Relative Tuning.

## Relative Tuning

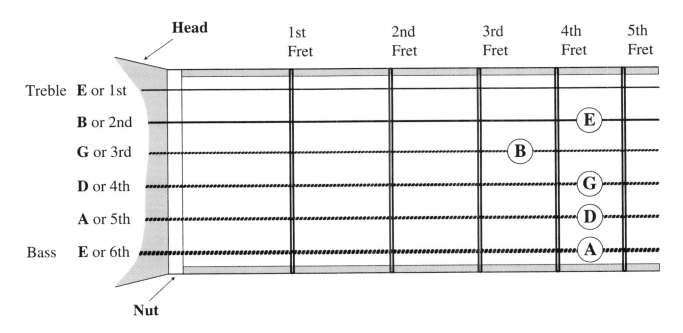

Press down where indicated, one at a time, following the instructions below

Estimate the pitch of the 6th string as near as possible to E or at least a comfortable pitch (not too high, as you might break other strings in tuning up).

Then, while checking the various positions on the above diagram, place a finger from your left hand on:

the 5th fret of the E or 6th string and **tune the open A** (or 5th string) to the note Ⓐ

the 5th fret of the A or 5th string and **tune the open D** (or 4th string) to the note Ⓓ

the 5th fret of the D or 4th string and **tune the open G** (or 3rd string) to the note Ⓖ

the 4th fret of the G or 3rd string and **tune the open B** (or 2nd string) to the note Ⓑ

the 5th fret of the B or 2nd string and **tune the open E** (or 1st string) to the note Ⓔ

## Scales In The Open Position

### C Major – Ascending

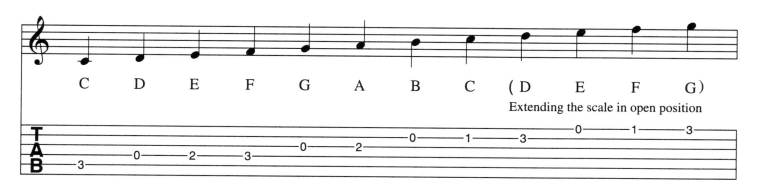

C D E F G A B C ( D E F G )

Extending the scale in open position

### C Major – Descending

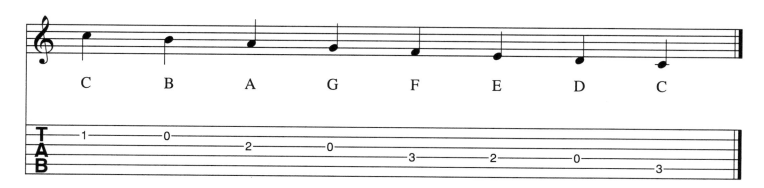

C B A G F E D C

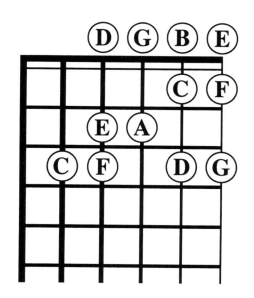

## G Major – Ascending

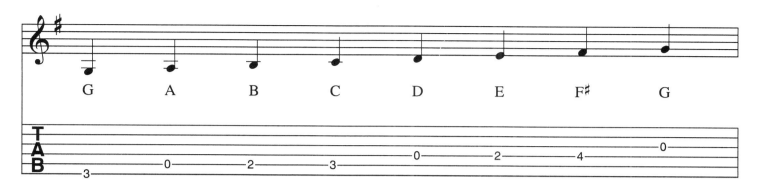

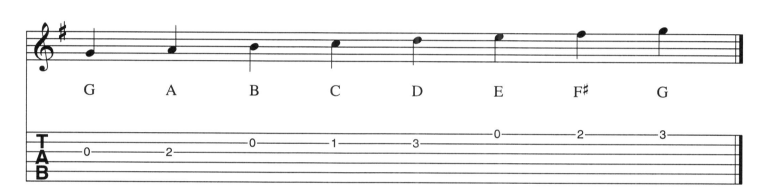

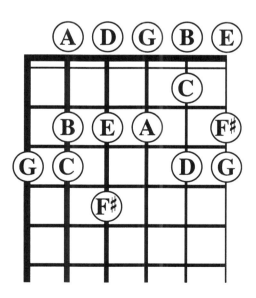

Note the key signature – this is the first
key we have encountered with a sharp sign (♯).

**D Major – Ascending**

D E F♯ G A B C♯ D (E F♯ G)

Extending the scale in open position

**D Major – Descending**

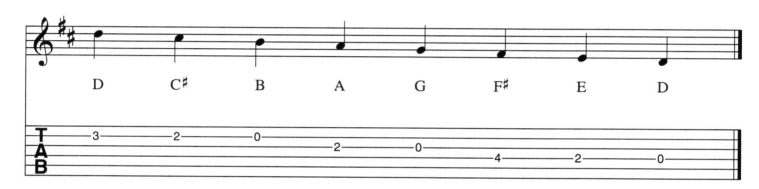

D C♯ B A G F♯ E D

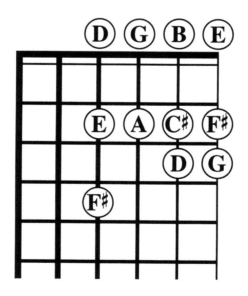

This scale has two sharpened notes in
the key signature – F sharp (♯) and C sharp (♯).

## A Major – Ascending

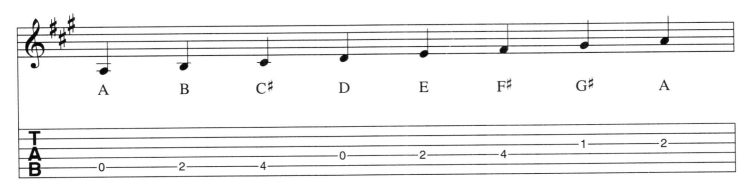

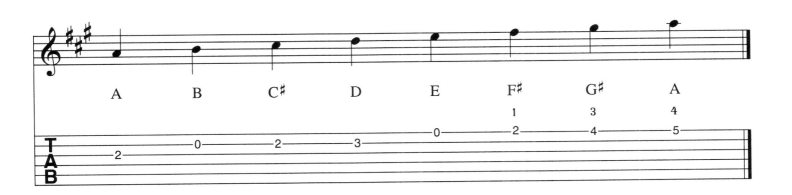

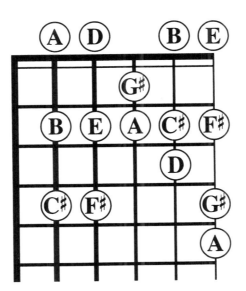

This scale moves higher than those previously encountered.
When you get to the top string, fret the F♯ with your first finger
so that the G♯ and A can be played with your third and fourth fingers.
This is called the second position.

## E Major – Ascending

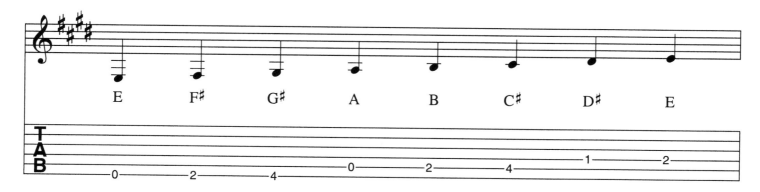

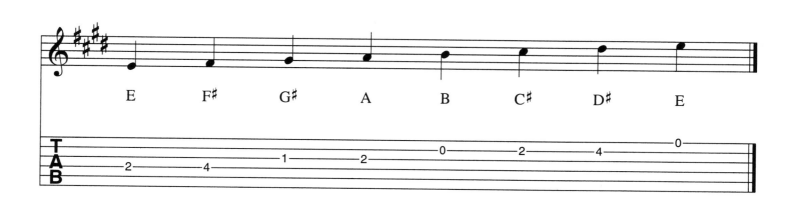

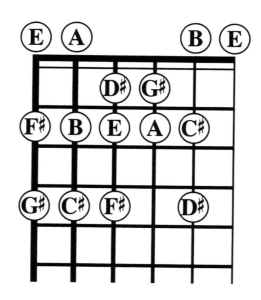

## A Natural Minor – Ascending

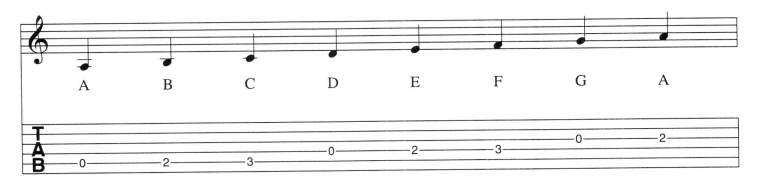

## A Natural Minor – Descending

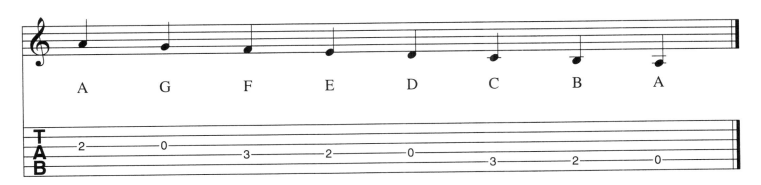

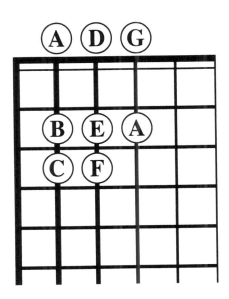

## A Melodic Minor – Ascending

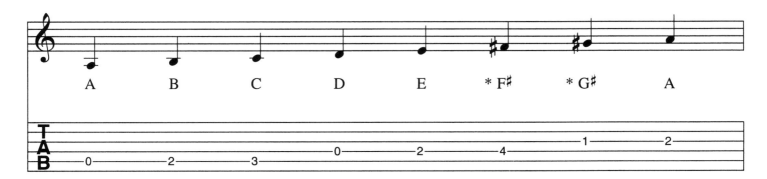

A    B    C    D    E    * F♯    * G♯    A

## A Melodic Minor – Descending

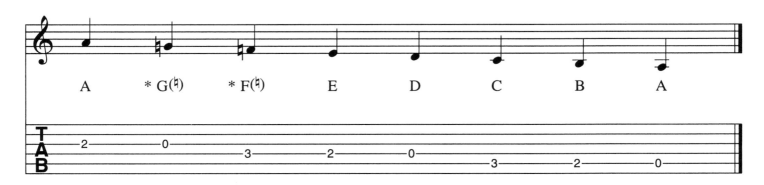

A    * G(♮)    * F(♮)    E    D    C    B    A

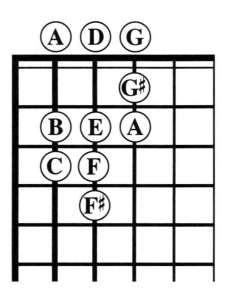

*In this scale the ascending pattern differs from the descending.
Jazz players often use just the ascending form.

## A Harmonic Minor – Ascending

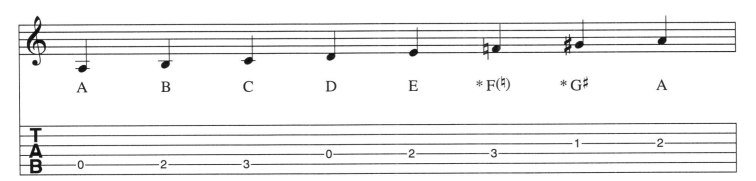

## A Harmonic Minor – Descending

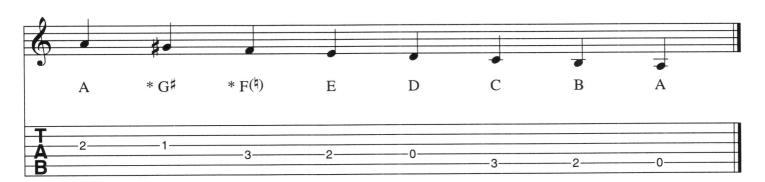

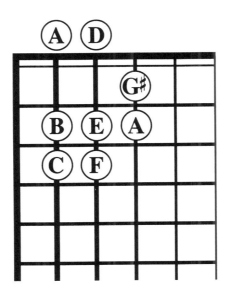

*The F is natural (♮) yet the G is sharpened (♯).
This interval gives a somewhat Eastern feeling.

## E Natural Minor – Ascending

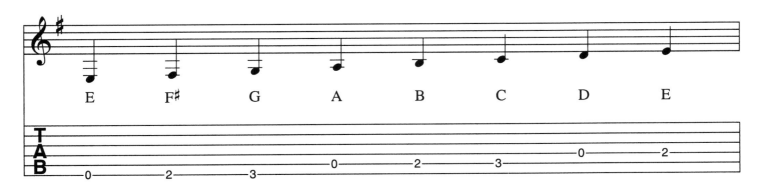

E  F#  G  A  B  C  D  E

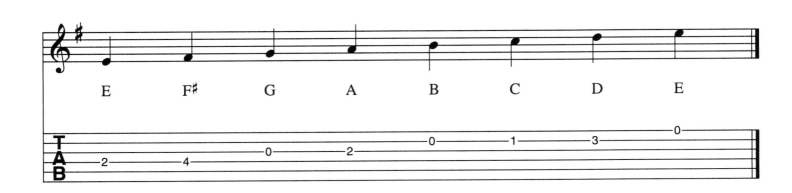

E  F#  G  A  B  C  D  E

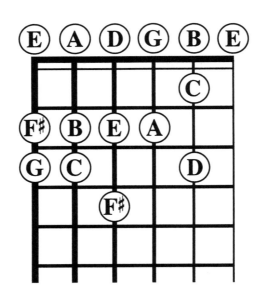

## E Melodic Minor – Ascending

## E Melodic Minor – Descending

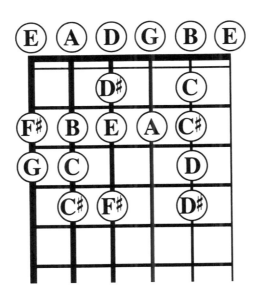

Note the difference between the ascending and descending
forms of the melodic minor scale.

## E Harmonic Minor – Ascending

## E Harmonic Minor – Descending

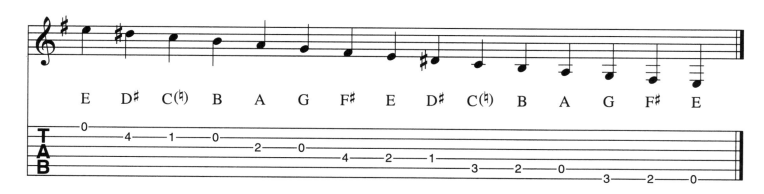

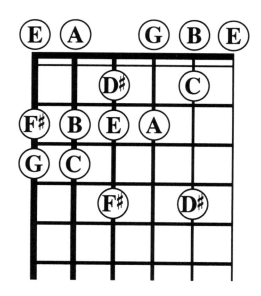

## B Natural Minor – Ascending

B  C♯  D  E  F♯  G  A  B  (C♯  D  E  F♯)

Extending the scale in open position

## B Natural Minor – Descending

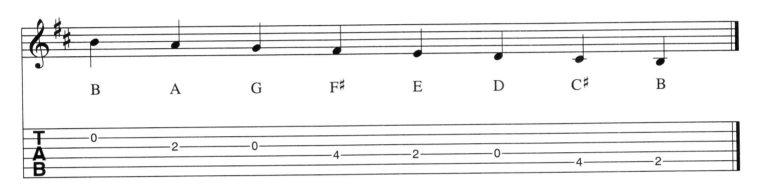

B  A  G  F♯  E  D  C♯  B

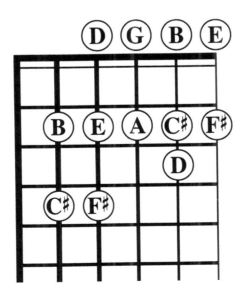

## F Major – Ascending

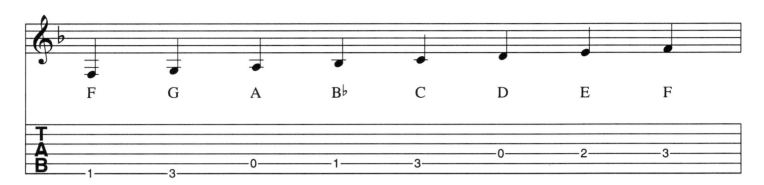

F     G     A     B♭     C     D     E     F

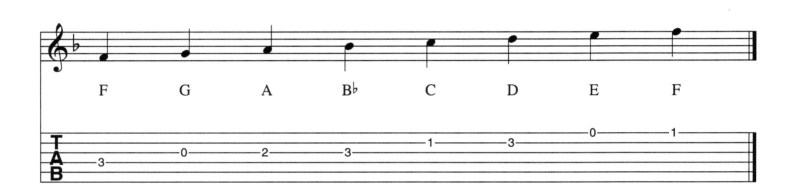

F     G     A     B♭     C     D     E     F

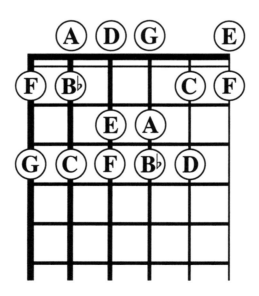

Note the key signature – this is the first
key we have encountered with a flat sign (♭).

## Bb Major – Ascending

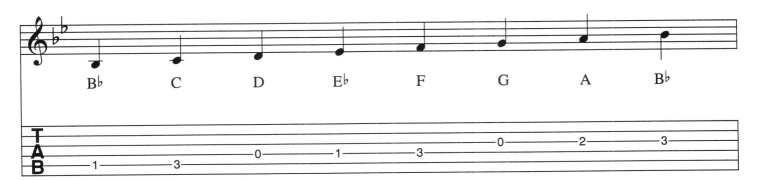

## Bb Major – Descending

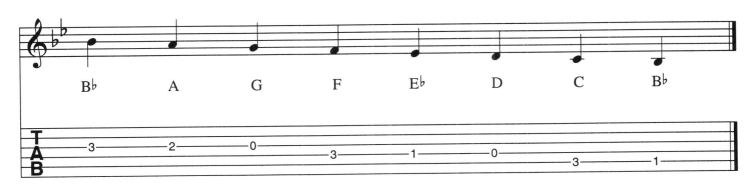

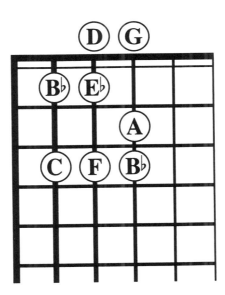

This scale has two flattened notes in
the key signature – B flat (♭) and E flat (♭).

## D Natural Minor – Ascending

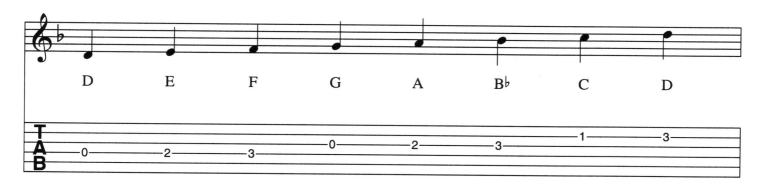

D  E  F  G  A  B♭  C  D

## D Natural Minor – Descending

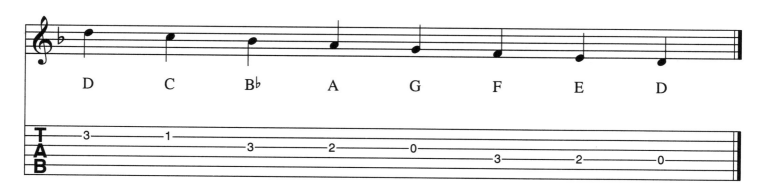

D  C  B♭  A  G  F  E  D

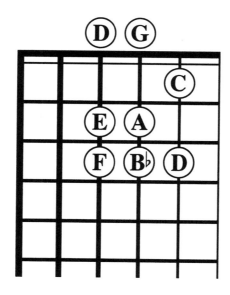

## G Natural Minor – Ascending

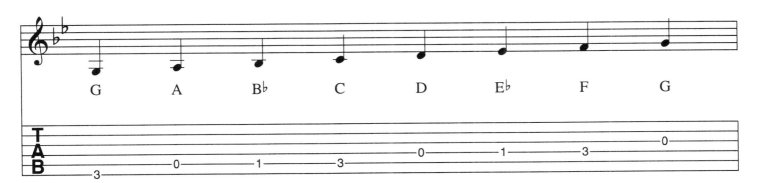

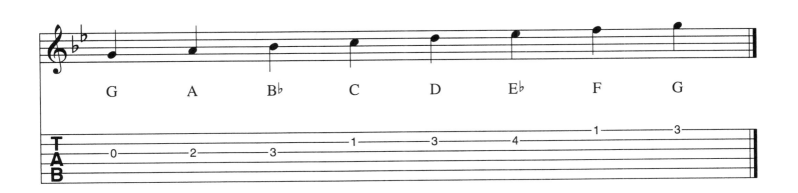

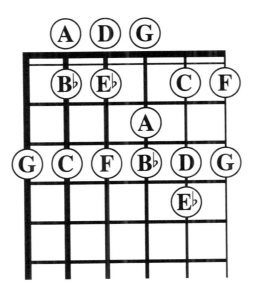

21

## E Minor Pentatonic – Ascending

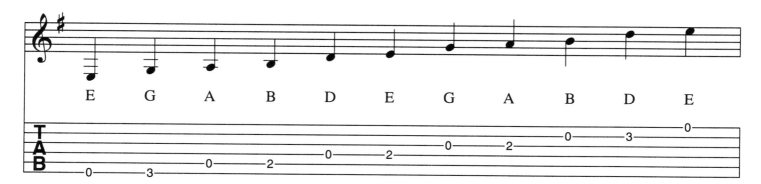

## E Minor Pentatonic – Descending

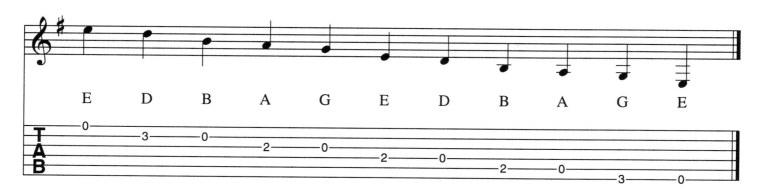

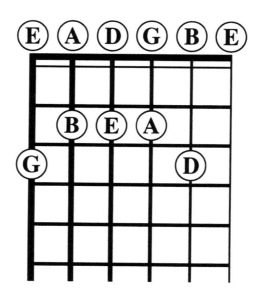

## E Major Pentatonic – Ascending

## E Major Pentatonic – Descending

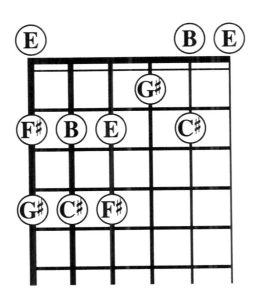

23

## A Minor Pentatonic – Ascending

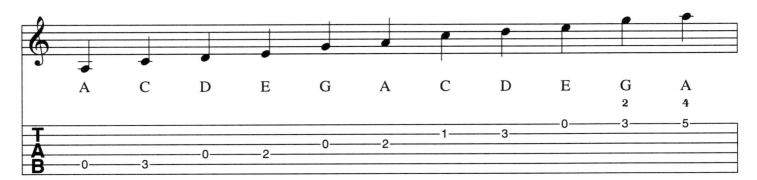

## A Minor Pentatonic – Descending

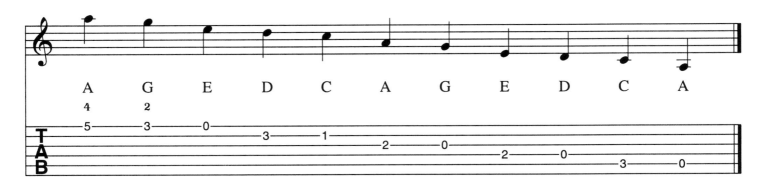

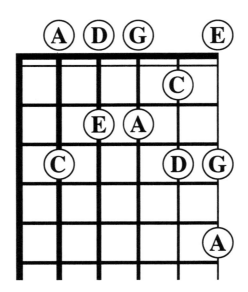

The two highest notes of this scale take us out of the open position
but the scale remains within fairly easy reach.

## A Major Pentatonic – Ascending

A    B    C♯    E    F♯    A    B    C♯    E    F♯    A
                                              *1    *4

## A Major Pentatonic – Descending

A    F♯    E    C♯    B    A    F♯    E    C♯    B    A
*4   *1

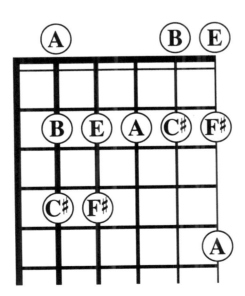

\* This scale uses the second position:
The first finger plays the 2nd fret, the fourth finger plays the 5th fret.

**25**

## B Minor Pentatonic – Ascending

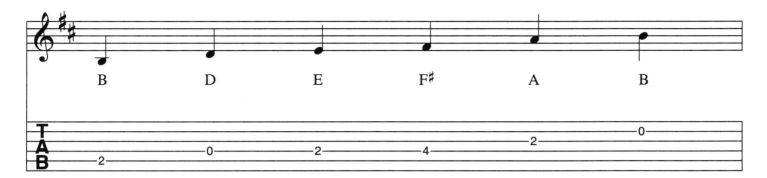

## B Minor Pentatonic – Descending

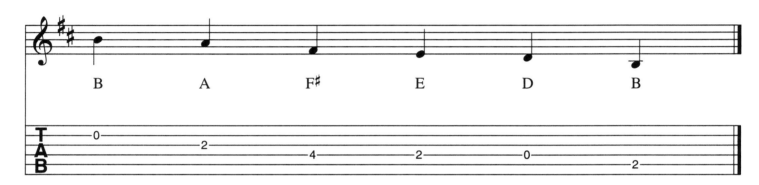

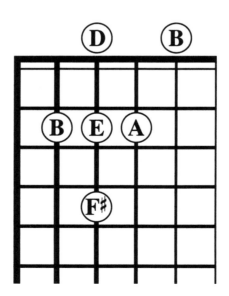

## B Major Pentatonic – Ascending

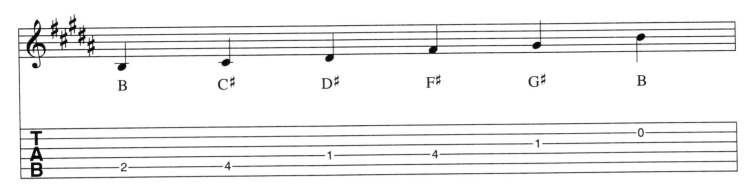

## B Major Pentatonic – Descending

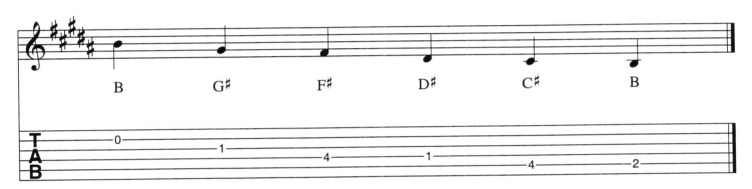

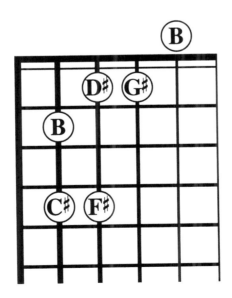

## C Minor Pentatonic – Ascending

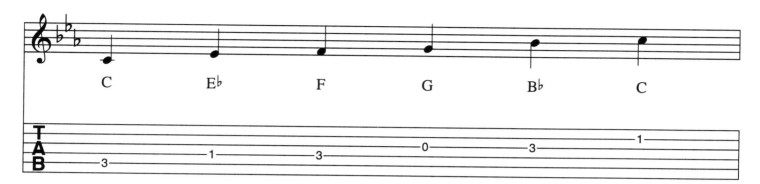

## C Minor Pentatonic – Descending

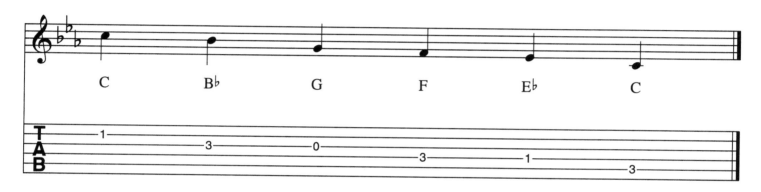

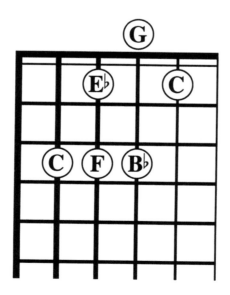

## C Major Pentatonic – Ascending

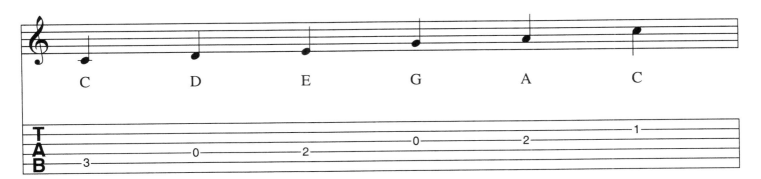

C  D  E  G  A  C

## C Major Pentatonic – Descending

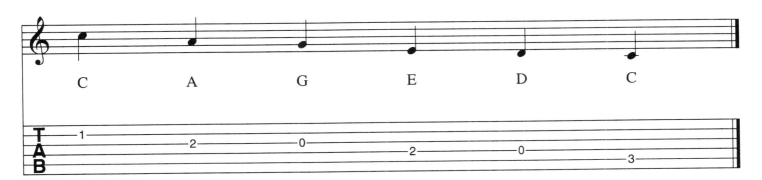

C  A  G  E  D  C

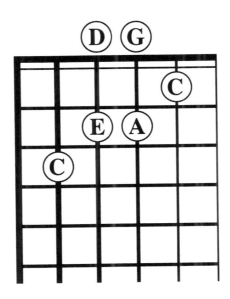

## D Minor Pentatonic – Ascending

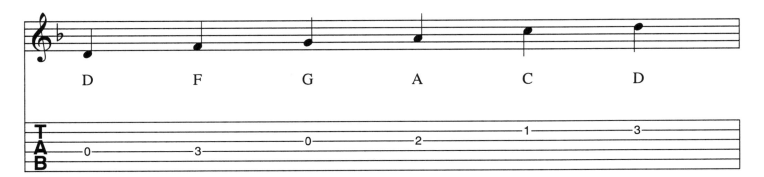

D     F     G     A     C     D

## D Minor Pentatonic – Descending

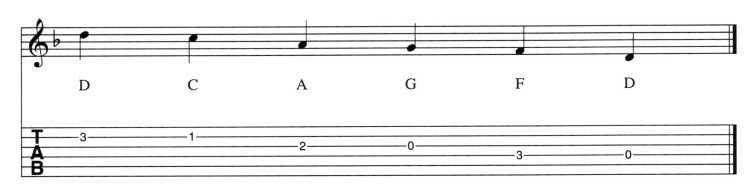

D     C     A     G     F     D

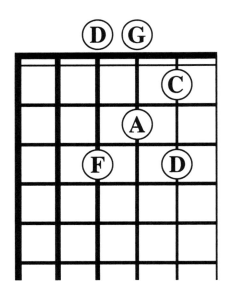

## D Major Pentatonic – Ascending

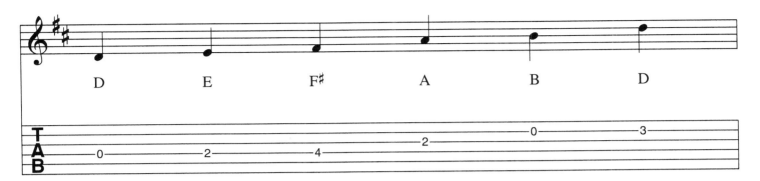

## D Major Pentatonic – Descending

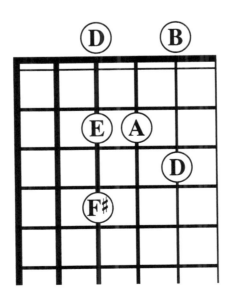

## G Minor Pentatonic – Ascending

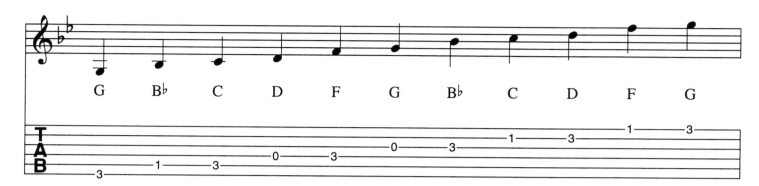

## G Minor Pentatonic – Descending

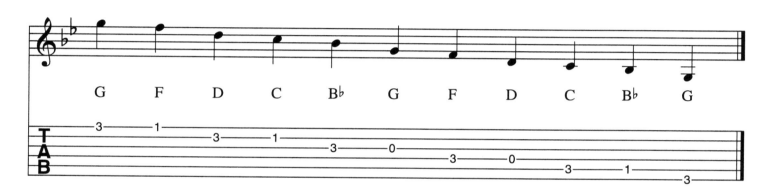

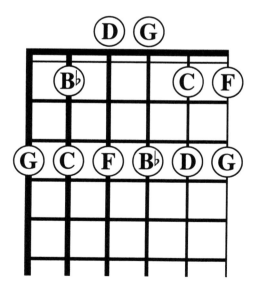

## G Major Pentatonic – Ascending

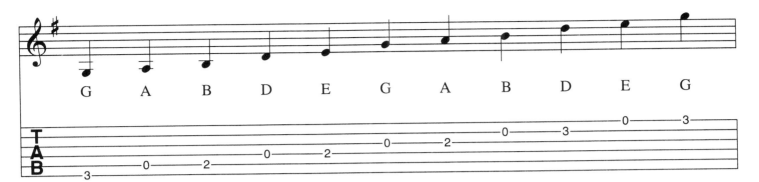

## G Major Pentatonic – Descending

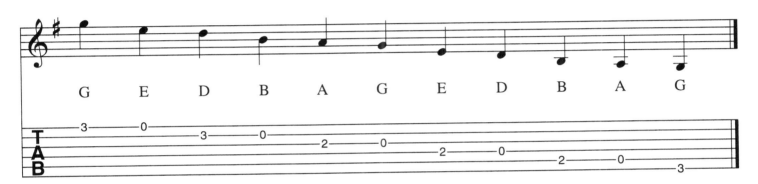

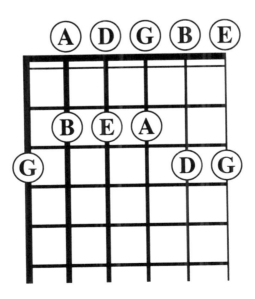

## D Blues Scale – Ascending

D    F    G    G♯    A    C    D

## D Blues Scale – Descending

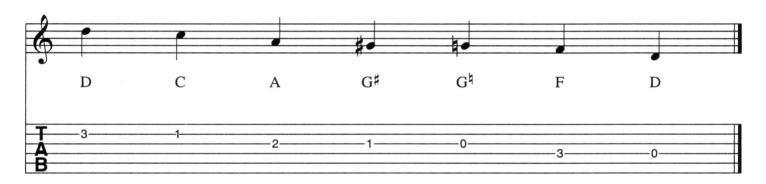

D    C    A    G♯    G♮    F    D

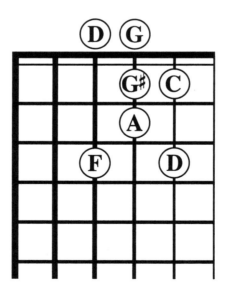

The Natural sign (♮) cancels the previous sharp sign.

## A Blues Scale – Open Position – Ascending

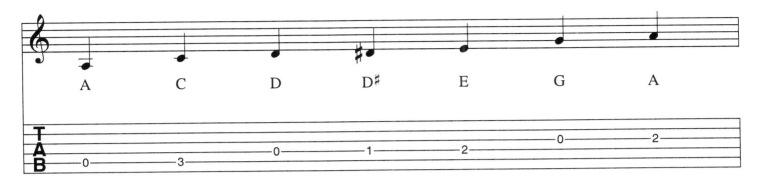

## A Blues Scale – Open Position – Descending

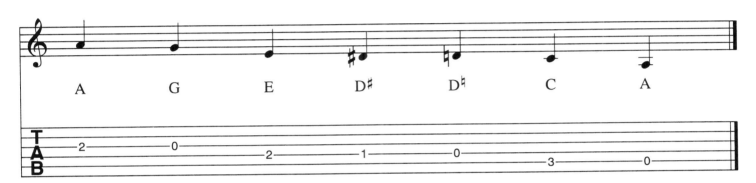

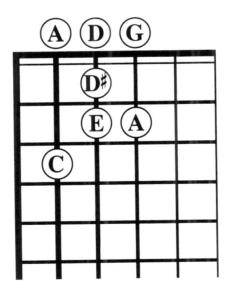

## E Blues Scale – Ascending

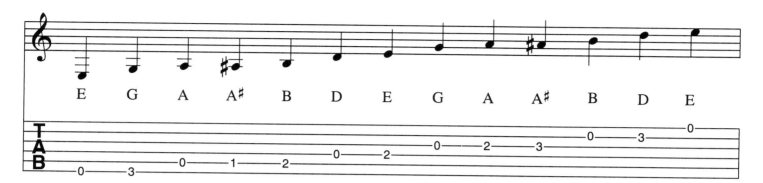

## E Blues Scale – Descending

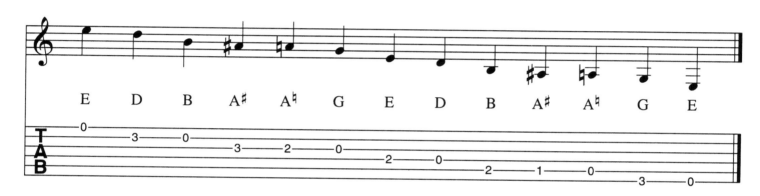

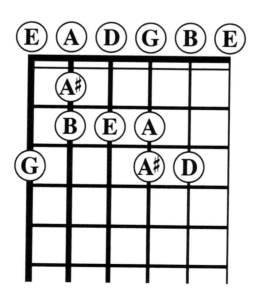

## Chromatic Scale From E – Ascending

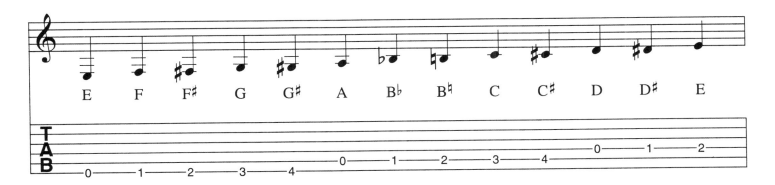

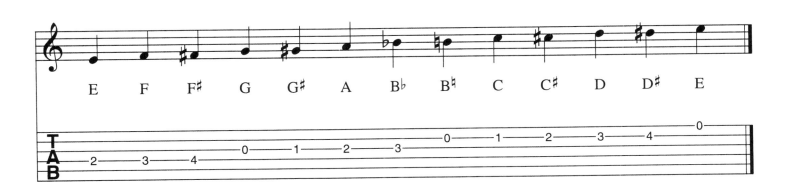

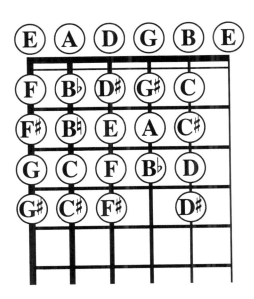

## Position Playing – Moving Up The Neck

### C Major – Ascending

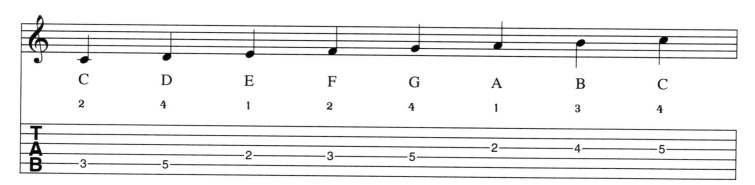

### C Major – Descending

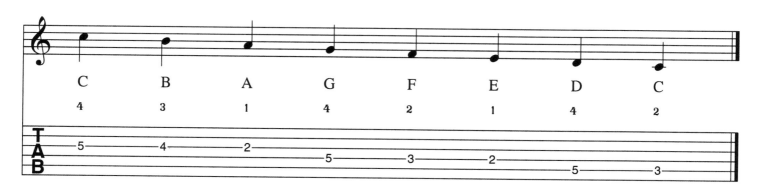

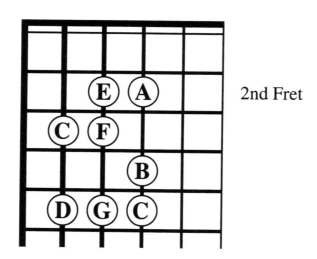

2nd Fret

This scale observes the one finger–one fret principle,
but the first finger is now placed in the second fret.

## G Major – Ascending

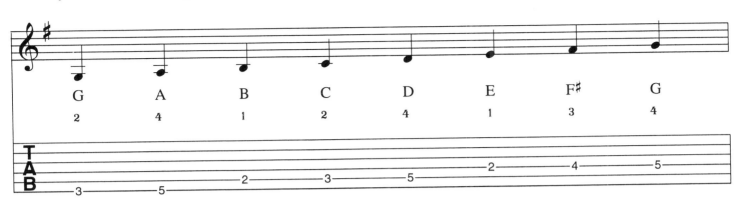

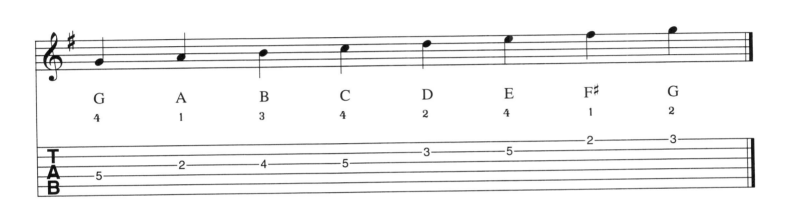

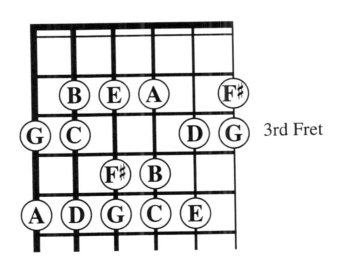

3rd Fret

This scale pattern can be moved up the neck to form other major scales.
The G Major scale pattern starting on A (2 frets higher) becomes the A Major scale.
This also applies to the C Major Scale on the previous page.

## A Blues Scale – 5th Position – Ascending

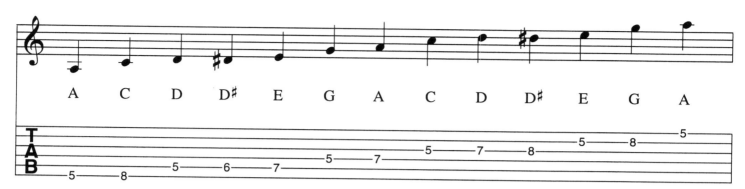

## A Blues Scale – 5th Position – Descending

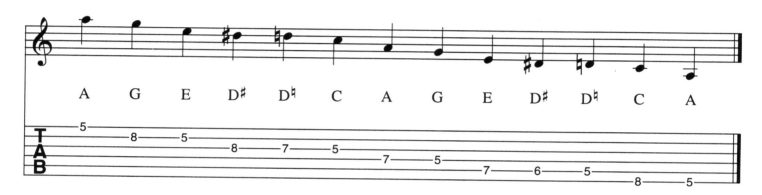

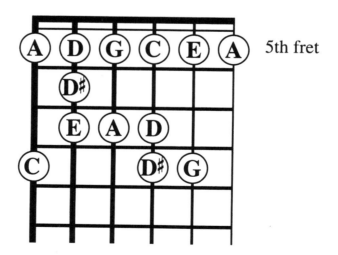

5th fret

Printed and bound in Great Britain by
Caligraving Limited Thetford Norfolk

1/01 (39208)

# contemporary •
# Magic &
# witchcraft

A COMPREHENSIVE EXAMINATION
Of MODERN WESTERN MAGIC

# contemporary • Magic & witchcraft

## SUSAN GREENWOOD

This edition is published by Southwater

Southwater is an imprint of Anness Publishing Ltd
Hermes House,
88–89 Blackfriars Road,
London SE1 8HA
tel. 020 7401 2077; fax 020 7633 9499
www.southwaterbooks.com; info@anness.com

© Anness Publishing Ltd 2003

This edition distributed in the UK by
The Manning Partnership Ltd,
6 The Old Dairy,
Melcombe Road,
Bath BA2 3LR;
tel. 01225 478 444; fax 01225 478 440;
sales@manning-partnership.co.uk

This edition distributed in the USA and Canada by
National Book Network,
4720 Boston Way,
Lanham,
MD 20706; tel. 301 459 3366; fax 301 459 1705;
www.nbnbooks.com

This edition distributed in Australia by
Pan Macmillan Australia,
Level 18, St Martins Tower,
31 Market St, Sydney, NSW 2000;
tel. 1300 135 113; fax 1300 135 103;
customer.service@macmillan.com.au

This edition distributed in New Zealand by
The Five Mile Press (NZ) Ltd,
PO Box 33–1071 Takapuna,
Unit 11/101–111 Diana Drive,
Glenfield, Auckland 10;
tel. (09) 444 4144; fax (09) 444 4518;
fivemilenz@clear.net.nz

A CIP catalogue record for this book is available from
the British Library.

Publisher: Joanna Lorenz
Managing Editor: Helen Sudell
Senior Editor: Joanne Rippin
Designer: Lesley Betts
Jacket Design: Andrew Nash
Typesetter: Diane Pullen

Previously published as part of a larger compendium,
*The Encyclopedia of Magic & Witchcraft*

10 9 8 7 6 5 4 3 2 1

# CONTENTS

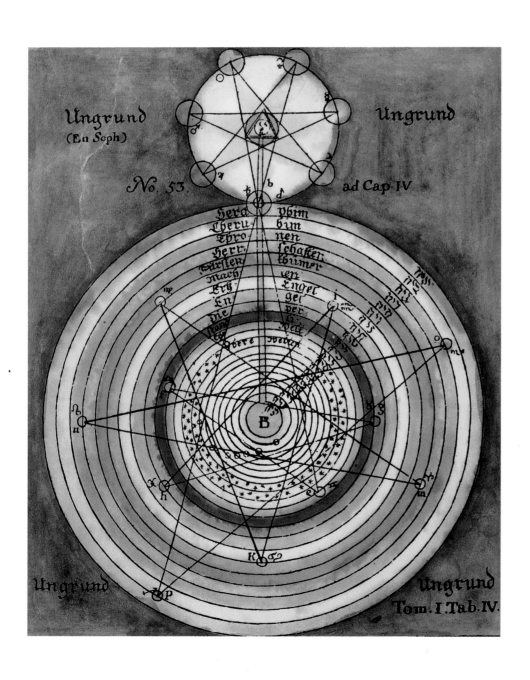

Ungrund
(En Soph)

Ungrund

No. 53.

ad Cap IV

Sera — phim
Cheru — bim
Thro — nen
Herr — schaften
Fürsten — thümer
Mach — ten
Ertz — Engel
En — gel
Die — ver
— schie —
— dene — Welt
obere Welt

Ungrund

Ungrund

Tom. I. Tab. IV.

# MODERN MAGIC

Magic today often receives a bad press: it is either associated with the work of the Devil, or it is reduced to popular entertainment in the form of conjuring tricks and sleight of hand. But as an expression of belief in an interconnecting world of spirit, magic is neither good nor evil in itself. It can be used in a variety of ways, depending on who is practising it. During the seventeenth century, as the Western world embraced scientific analysis, magic was increasingly seen as irrational, and those who practised the occult arts went underground. Many secret societies – such as the Rosicrucians and Freemasons – were formed, and modern magical practices still reflect this history.

# MAGIC'S ANCIENT ROOTS

Since the earliest times, human beings have sought to communicate with, and control, the world around them. Ideas about what we now call magic probably developed naturally from people living together in social groups – through intimate relationships, giving birth to children, mourning the death of a clan or tribe member – and also from the shaman's spiritual link with the animals that were hunted. The idea that there is a subtle, invisible essence that comes from all beings – rocks, stones, plants, fungi and animals as well as human beings – is a basic principle of magical belief. People in different cultures from all around the world have attempted to tap into and control this essence or force.

*Haloes are not confined to Christianity – the spiritual aura of the Buddha surrounded his body as well as his head.*

In many spiritual traditions the human body is seen to be made up of a spirit body (which may be called a soul, an etheric body or an aura) as well as a physical body. The spirit body is often viewed as a life-force. It is thought to be subject to damage, leakage or disease, or even psychic vampirism. It is said that a person's spiritual development can be determined by the condition of their spirit body. A halo – the light that appears around a saint's head – marks advancement. The spiritual aura of the Buddha was said to extend for 320 km (200 miles).

Magicians seek to work directly with the spirit body and use it to link up with the hidden energies of all manner of beings in the cosmos: from the earth energies of trees, through techniques of visualization to invoke gods and goddesses, to wider planetary influences, of the sun and the moon, for example. Each of the magical tradition works in a different way.

The ways that magicians work today have been influenced by ideas from the past. Modern magical ideas were born in the Renaissance. "Renaissance" means rebirth, and the magicians of the time focused on uniting the individual soul with God in terms of what is now called Neoplatonism. The work most influential to Renaissance magicians was the *Corpus*

*Hermeticum*, a composite of individual writings by various unknown authors, which was probably of Greek origin and not, as was believed in the Renaissance, the work of an Egyptian priest called Hermes Trismegistus. The works are philosophical and concern magical and astrological ways of making talismans to draw down the powers of the stars, and record the means by which individual souls can find divine knowledge without the aid of a personal god or saviour. Magicians need to try and understand the hidden forces in nature: of external phenomena and within themselves.

Alchemy was highly popular during the fourteenth to the seventeenth centuries, as shown in Shakespeare's Sonnet 33:

> *Full many a glorious*
> *morning have I seen*
> *Flatter the mountain-tops*
> *with sovereign eye,*
> *Kissing with golden face*
> *the meadows green,*
> *Gilding pale streams with*
> *heavenly alchemy.*

*The haloes that surround the heads of the Christian saints are a sign of their special holiness.*

The sonnet suggests a mystical, alchemical link between the natural elements of mountain, meadows and streams.

Alchemy became the greatest passion of the age, combining the search for the philosopher's stone, which it was believed held the power to transmute base metals into gold, with an internal (esoteric) spiritual quest. Alchemy was viewed as an art that would lead to transmutation. It was considered an embryonic science – a protochemistry; early alchemists used laboratories for their experiments and study, and made a number of discoveries that contributed to the development of chemistry.

Alchemists conducted experiments with metals and other substances and interpreted their results using astrology, cabbalism and herbalism, frequently employing the language of mystical Christian symbolism.

This was also a time when great store was set by divination. One famous diviner was Nostradamus (1503–66). Born Michel de Notredame, he came from a Jewish family in St Rémy-en-Provence and graduated as a doctor of medicine in Montpellier. He worked with plague victims in Marseilles and Avignon, but he refused to bleed his patients, as was the usual procedure. On a couple of occasions he had to flee the area because the Inquisition thought he was a wizard.

Nostradamus' prophecies were composed with the aid of magical, astrological and cabbalistic books and were published in two parts, in 1555 and 1568. Both Napoleon Bonaparte and Adolf Hitler, in their respective centuries, believed that their careers had been foreseen in Nostradamus' predictions, and it is also said that he predicted the French Revolution of 1789.

During the seventeenth century, the rise of scientific rationalism and Protestantism drove magic underground. Scientific rationalism was a mechanistic philosophy that viewed the world as a machine. As Protestantism grew, it attempted to take out of Christian practice what it viewed as magical elements – for example the Catholic dependence on the powers of saints'

*A contemporary portrait of Nostradamus, whose prophecies are still read avidly today.*

*A painting from the late fifteenth century of an alchemy master preparing ingredients.*

relics. During this period, these two developments in thought meant that people who practised magic did so in secret, and tended to be attracted to underground societies such as the Rosicrucians or the Freemasons.

*Left: Conjurors were an accepted part of everyday life between the fourteenth and seventeenth centuries.*

# Neoplatonism

The philosophy of Neoplatonism originated with Plotinus (c.AD205–270). It was a synthesis of earlier philosophical thought and religious beliefs, combining alchemy and magic to provide not only an image of the universe and the human place within it, but also a method of spiritual salvation. The 'One' as a deity is the source of all goodness and reality. The One is the source from which everything flows, and the gradual dispersion of the original unity results in multiplicity and matter (which is sometimes equated with evil). Human imperfection, which is due to a flaw or the Fall, stems from the soul's remoteness from the One. The soul is longing to return to completeness, but as the One is beyond description and cannot be reached through rational thinking, it has to be approached through ecstatic contemplative absorption. The soul has many levels: the highest is intellectual thought, and the lowest is the animating principle of the material universe. All humans have all aspects of soul within them and have to choose whether to wake the higher elements or remain immersed in the concerns of the material body.

# THE MYTH OF ATLANTIS

Those who continued to work with magic, despite the movement against it, attempted to create meaning by looking for significant connections between things, and this frequently involved the use of myths. A myth is a sacred story that is shared by a group of people who find their most important meanings in it. In Western cultures mythology is often equated with fairy stories, the "unreal" or even falsehood, and contrasted with history, which is associated with the truth. However, myth has played an important part in magic by explaining how the world came to be formed, and by marking out significant relationships with ancestors and other beings. The myth of Atlantis is especially important to Western magicians. It is said to be a sunken island that occupied most of the area of the Atlantic Ocean, and is the place from which the peoples of Europe arose.

*The kings of Atlantis were said to be descended from the sons of Poseidon, the sea god.*

## THE ORIGINS

The myth of Atlantis has a very important position in Western magic. The name "Atlantis" conjures up visions of a wonderful land of beauty and plenty, a utopian society where peace and justice reigned; a golden country lying in the midst of a wide blue sea. The legend concerns the story of an ancient island civilization, in conflict with Athens and Egypt, which vanished in a day and a night due to spiritual disaster. It was Plato (c.428–347BC) who first wrote about the myth in *Timaeus*, telling how a mighty power had once come out of the Atlantic Ocean. The size and position of lost Atlantis was revealed to the Athenian statesman and poet Solon by an Egyptian priest in about 590BC. The priest described Atlantis as a kingdom that had been much larger than Libya and Asia Minor put together, which had, some 9,000 years before, been situated beyond the Pillars of Hercules at the western end of the Mediterranean Sea. Its armies had once conquered most of the countries of the Mediterranean:

*The idea of the lost land of Atlantis came from Classical Greece, where students of philosophy would discuss utopian societies and ideal states, which were governed by democratic principles or benign dictators.*

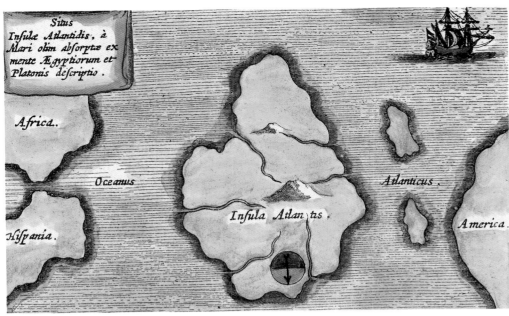

*Now in this island of Atlantis there was a great and wonderful empire which had rule over the whole island and several others ... This vast power, gathered into one, endeavoured to subdue ... the whole of the region ... She was pre-eminent in courage and military skill, and was the leader of the Hellenes. And when the rest fell off from her, being compelled to stand alone, after having undergone the very extremity of dangers, she defeated and triumphed over the invaders, and preserved from slavery those who were not yet subjugated, and generously liberated all the rest of us who dwelt within the pillars. But afterwards there occurred violent earthquakes and floods; and in a single day and night of misfortune all your warlike men in a body sank into the earth, and the island of Atlantis in like manner disappeared in the depths of the sea.*

*A seventeenth-century map of the imagined island of Atlantis.*

*Ya-uli, an Atlantean high priest, according to theosophists Besant and Leadbeater.*

In *Critias*, Plato describes how, after the Creation, the gods divided up the world:

*Athena acquired Greece, and set up the first Athenian state, and the sea-god Poseidon received Atlantis. Poseidon divided the island between his sons to rule, and it was these kings and their descendants who built the city of Atlantis. The kings met every fifth or sixth year to discuss affairs of state after sacrificing a bull during an elaborate ceremony. For a long time the Atlanteans were virtuous but gradually they became corrupt and greedy, and Zeus decided to punish them. The gods were called to a meeting but there ...*

Plato's dialogue ends in mid-sentence, so nothing more is known.

## THE GOLDEN AGE

The enthusiasm among magicians for the legend of Atlantis indicates a nostalgia for a lost world and a primal state of wholeness before humans lost contact with their spiritual source. The myth forms an ideal vision of a golden age, a time in the past where there was complete social and spiritual harmony: a Garden of Eden before the Fall, when humans were in touch with divinity.

Many modern magicians search for ways to reconnect with this ideal state of existence and, at the same time, work with their internal spiritual selves. Some claim to be in telepathic communication with the erstwhile inhabitants of Atlantis; others have memories of previous incarnations spent on the island. A profusion of books appears each year on Atlantis and a popular theme among Atlantists is that the civilizations of the New and Old Worlds shared a common cultural origin that sprang from it. This would explain common myths, symbols and even language.

# Atlantis and the occult

Atlantis is seen to be the home of the initiates of a secret occult tradition, which has been passed on through various sects and secret magical societies, from the Templars, the Rosicrucians, the Freemasons and various occult schools. Some of these schools have claimed to have reconstructed the entire history of Atlantis by means of spirit messages. Edgar Cayce, a well-known American psychic Christian, born in 1877, was disturbed to find out that in trance he had delivered the history of humanity dating back to Atlantis. In a science-fiction like epic, he said that Atlantis had been inhabited by a civilization whose technologies were based on the power of crystals.

*An Atlantean pyramid, as imagined in 1923 by Manly P. Hall.*

# THE TAROT

The methods used to reconnect with the spiritual world are various, but one that is central to many magical practices is the set of cards called the tarot. The origin of cartomancy, or divination by cards, is unknown. The practice was established in Italy, France and Germany by the late fourteenth century and has been attributed to the Knights Templar or the Gypsies, but both are unlikely. Evidence suggests that the idea of playing cards came from China, Korea or India but that the designs of the tarot came from Europe.

*A.E. Waite, the co-producer with Pamela Coleman Smith of an extremely popular tarot deck.*

The tarot consists of 78 cards, and these are made up of 56 cards of the lesser arcana, and 22 cards of the greater arcana. The lesser arcana is divided into four suits: batons, cups, swords and coins. Each suit has four court cards – King, Queen, Knight and Page – and ten numbered cards. The greater arcana depicts certain symbols and images that are numbered in sequence and range from the Fool (who is unnumbered or zero) to the World (number 21). The images on the cards represent the total energies of the universe, and some magicians say that they concern

*Four examples of the designs for the Waite-Coleman tarot deck.*

initiation into the mysteries. They represent the stages of a life journey and, by solving the riddle that each card presents, they offer an opportunity for spiritual development. The tarot is said to speak in symbols, the language of the unconscious, and, when approached in the right manner, to open doors into the hidden reaches of the soul.

The French occultist Eliphas Lévi (1810–75), whose first work on magic, *Dogme et Rituel de la Haute Magie*, was published in 1855, linked the tarot to the esoteric system of the cabbala and the

*The magician Eliphas Lévi, who first linked the tarot to the esoteric system of the cabbala.*

22 letters of the Hebrew alphabet. He also connected the four suits of the lesser arcana to the four elements, and to the four letters of the divine name of God. This had a great influence on later occultists. Lévi was also largely responsible for the revival of interest in the nineteenth-century theory of astral light as a fluid force that permeated everything, and which the magician must learn to control.

The Hermetic Order of the Golden Dawn adopted Lévi's system but assigned the cards in a slightly different way; they also linked the 22 cards of the greater arcana with the 22 paths of the cabbala, and added the signs of the zodiac and the planets to combine various systems into one.

## TAROT DECKS

The three most important tarot decks of the modern era are those of the Golden Dawn, A. E. Waite and Aleister Crowley. The magician A. E. Waite and the artist Pamela Coleman Smith produced an extremely popular version of the tarot pack in 1910. In 1944, Aleister Crowley (1875–1947), an ex-Golden Dawn member, published *The Book of Thoth*, and directed the artist Lady Frieda Harris to illustrate a pack according to this interpretation. All three decks were dependent on a set of tarot papers called Book T, which were issued to members of the inner lodge of the Hermetic Order of the Golden Dawn. These papers suggested that the key to the tarot was found in the cabbala and that the tarot was an external symbol of the underlying pattern of the cosmos. The book includes lines from the Revelation of Saint John the Divine and suggests that the tarot is the book referred to in this work, and that only those who have been initiated into the secret mysteries can fully understand the tarot. It begins:

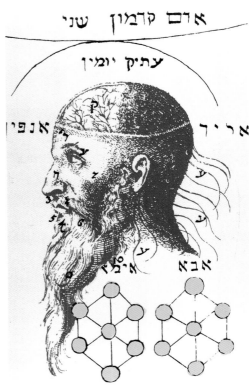

*Hru the Great Angel is Set over the operations of the Secret Wisdom
What thou seest write in a Book, and send it unto the Seven Abodes that are in Assiah.
And I saw in the right hand of Him that sat upon the Throne a book sealed with Seven Seals. And I saw a strong Angel proclaiming with a loud voice.
Who is worthy to open the Books and to loose the seals thereof?*

Only an initiate is worthy of loosening the seals and understanding the true mysteries of the tarot.

*Tarot cards are used today in many forms of divination. Said to reach the deepest parts of a person's subconscious, they can give personal and spiritual insight.*

*The cabbala was originally an esoteric aspect of Judaism; today it is interpreted more widely.*

# The cabbala

The cabbala, originally the inner and mystical aspect of Judaism, provides a framework for many magical systems – such as the tarot, astrology and alchemy – and is thought to represent every force manifested in the universe. Essentially a form of Neoplatonism, Godhead is seen to be brought down to humanity via the spheres (sephiroth) of the Tree of Life. In cabbalistic cosmology, Creation, like the descent of pure light, works downwards from AYIN (God transcendent) to EN SOF (immanent God) through to AYIN SOF OR (limitless light), which becomes manifest in the ten spheres of the cabbala. The relationships of the spheres represent the whole of existence – they are both attributes of God and aspects of human experience – and offer human beings the means of attaining spiritual oneness with the Ultimate.

The Tree of Life is used as a framework for meditation (on the qualities of a particular sphere, for example), or for "pathworking", an active meditation that engages the imagination, while in a state of trance, on the pathways interlinking the spheres. Cabbalistic magical training concerns training the mind through visualization – the creation of images using the imagination.

Tarot cards are often used to represent the energies and attributes of a particular path on the Tree of Life. Thus by working on the Tree of Life a magician is said to be able to reach deeper and unknown parts of his or her subconsciousness; this is said to lead to greater self understanding and also spiritual revelation. The Tree of Life represents an inner "map" of the cosmos and a way of uniting with God.

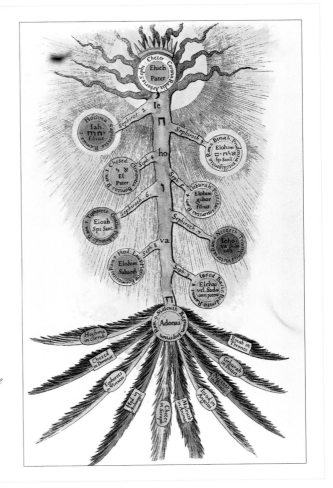

*There are many interpretations of the cabbalistic Tree of Life. This one is from Kircher's* Oedipus Aegyptiacus, *1652. More modern ones have distinct pathways linking the spheres to aid meditation.*

# MAGICAL SOCIETIES

The word "occult" conveys the ideas of secrecy and hidden knowledge; a central component of magical organizations in the past was the transmission of esoteric wisdom through initiation rites. During the seventeenth century there was a fascination with secret societies and it was at this time that Rosicrucianism and Freemasonry were established. Rosicrucianism was founded on myths and allegories that were based on the restoration of a divine state through inner experience. The Rosicrucians used alchemy and cabbala to achieve this divine state. In similar fashion, the spiritual aspects of Freemasonry are concerned with making contact with a divine source through the symbolism of the Temple of Solomon. The nineteenth-century Theosophical Society was based on the idea that there was an ancient spiritual science concerned with the mysteries of the interaction between human beings and God. Likewise, the later nineteenth-century Hermetic Order of the Golden Dawn – a synthesis of the practices and traditions of Rosicrucianism, Freemasonry and Theosophy – was also focused on a mystical union with divinity. All these magical societies sought a higher spiritual knowledge or experience as a means of uniting with God.

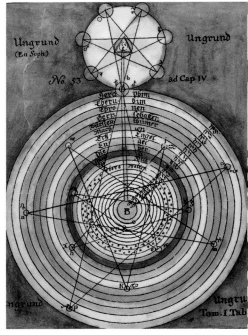

*A Rosicrucian diagram of the spiritual realm in relation to the descent of the reincarnating soul.*

## THE ROSICRUCIANS

The years 1614 and 1615 saw the publication of two short pamphlets, the *Fama* and the *Confessio*, which became known as the Rosicrucian manifestos. They were utopian myths about bringing humanity back to its divine state before the Fall, and made the stirring announcement of the dawn of a new enlightenment. Their message was framed in an allegory in which the central idea was the spiritual opening to divine inner experience. According to this allegory, a Rosicrucian brother had discovered a large brass nail during building alterations. When the nail was removed it revealed a door behind, on which was written the words *"POST CCXX ANOS PATEBO"* ("After 120 years I shall reopen"). When the door was eventually opened,

*... there appeared to our sight a Vault of Seven Sides ... although the Sun never shined in that Vault, nevertheless it was enlightened with another Sun ... and was situated in the upper part in the centre of the*

*ceiling. In the midst ... was a round altar, covered with a plate of brass, and thereon this engraven "I have made this Tomb a compendium of the Universe". Round the brim were the words "Jesus is all things to me". In the middle were four figures, enclosed in circles, whose circumscription was (1) Nowhere a Vacuum (2) The Burden of the Law (3) The Liberty of the Gospel (4) The Untouched Glory of God. Now as we had not yet seen the body of our careful and wise Father, we therefore removed the altar aside; then we lifted up a strong plate of brass and found a fair and worthy body, whole and unconsumed ... In his hand he held the book T, the which next unto our Bible is our greatest treasure.*

Behind the walls of the tomb the brethren found books, magical mirrors, bells and even "ever-burning lamps". The first two manifestos were connected with a third publication, *The Chymical*

*Right: The Rosicrucian Rosy Cross as depicted by the nineteenth-century Hermetic Order of the Golden Dawn.*

*Wedding of Christian Rosencreutz*, written in 1616 by Johann Valentin Andreae. This concerned another allegory, this time based on the mystic marriage of the soul. By setting forth an alternative to the Jesuit Order, the Rosicrucians promised

a prophetic return to a state of paradise through the use of alchemy, cabbala and evangelical piety. Their aim was to promote a programme of research and reform of the sciences.

## FREEMASONRY

The origins of Freemasonry are unclear; it has been linked with Rosicrucianism and the Knights Templar, but nothing is known for certain.

The history of Freemasonry is entwined with the Hermetic and cabbalistic traditions, which were studied in England during the second half of the sixteenth century. In 1717 the Grand Lodge was formed, this used a system of symbolism based on the society of stonemasons called the Operative Mason's Craft, together with ideas from the Western mystical tradition. In ancient Greek culture, much effort had been made to capture the gods' characters in stone structures, and this decorative architecture influenced the Roman architect Vitruvius, who wanted to capture the spiritual essence of building to demonstrate that the human being and the building were constructed according to the same plan. The mystical tradition that Vitruvius discovered was handed down through the medieval guilds of stonemasons, and preserved by a small group within the trade.

In the view of Freemasons, the complete human being is made up of a body, a psyche or soul, a spirit and a contact with his divine source. The human psyche contains four levels, which reflect the larger four-level structure described above. In specific terms, Freemasonry represents the psyche with the Temple of Solomon, which it describes as a three-storey temple within which one can be conscious of the presence of divinity.

Freemasonry consists of three basic degrees: Entered Apprentice; Fellow Craft; and Master Mason; as well as "higher" or "side" degrees of the *Rose Croix*. In addition there is the Knight of the Pelican and Eagle and Sovereign, Prince Rose Croix of Heredom, Grand

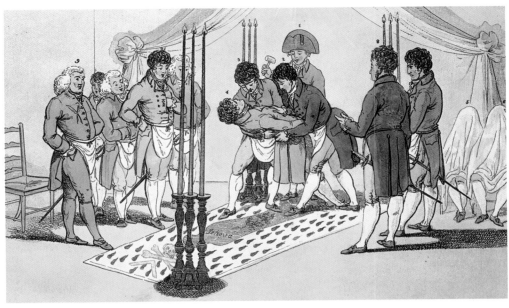

*A nineteenth-century depiction of a Freemasonry initiation.*

*The ceremonies and symbols of Freemasonry as shown in the frontispiece to a nineteenth-century book on its history.*

Elected Knight Kadosh and Knight of Black and White Eagle. There are also many offices within a lodge such as Worshipful Master Deacons and Wardens, which are positions rather than levels of initiation. In Britain, Masonry was responsible for keeping alive the occult tradition from the sixteenth to the nineteenth century. Freemasonry has had an important influence on contemporary magical practices, mainly the Hermetic Order of the Golden Dawn.

# THE THEOSOPHICAL SOCIETY

The nineteenth century was an age of independent spiritual teachers in a time of declining established religion, when many people were looking to find a single key to solve the mysteries of the universe. Among these was Emanuel Swedenborg (1688–1772), who developed a theory of correspondences and a view of the universe as a harmonious whole, which was only temporarily disturbed by sin. This was coupled with a belief in the accessibility of the spiritual world together with a trust in the reality of a new political and religious dispensation that would bring together the various orders of science and religion and would combine them with the imagination.

The theory of magnetism propounded by Anton Mesmer (1734–1815) was also popular. This was based on the notion that the human body was surrounded by a magnetic force, which a healer could detect for therapeutic purposes. The movement that became know as spiritualism also attracted many people who believed that the spirits of the dead could be channelled by mediums who had special psychic powers.

## HELENA BLAVATSKY

This was the climate of ideas from which the Theosophical Society emerged. It was founded by Helena Petrovna Blavatsky (1831–91) and Henry Steel Olcott (1832–1907) in 1875, and it played a major part in spreading occult ideas at the turn of the nineteenth century. At its inception its objectives were to form a universal brotherhood of humanity without distinction of race, creed, sex, caste or colour; to encourage the study of comparative religion, philosophy and science; and to investigate unexplained laws of nature and the powers latent in humans. These last two objectives were later developed by HPB, as she was popularly known, in *Isis Unveiled*, subtitled "A Master-Key to the Mysteries of Ancient and Modern Science and Theology" (1877), in which she attempted to integrate science and religion. At this stage the theosophical doctrine was still in its formative stages, but was being structured around the idea that there was an ancient, secret spiritual

*Anton Mesmer, the Austrian physician who popularized the idea that the human body was surrounded by a magnetic force, a belief that still holds sway in many different natural therapies.*

science known to a brotherhood of adepts who would transmit it to select individuals. Blavatsky claimed that science was called "magic" in the far-off days and explored the primary force of nature's mysteries within a universe of cyclic phenomena. These mysteries were in essence the interaction between God and humanity.

The core of Blavatsky's theosophy was that "Man must know himself" and that ordinary religion was just dogma with no scientific foundation. Science, too, was unsatisfactory because it ignored the unseen being. For Blavatsky, the whole was constituted of both the visible and the invisible, the facts of nature being grasped from within the human body as well as without. She was an adamant anti-Darwinian, believing in the spiritual evolution of the psyche rather than the physical evolution of primates. The role of theosophy was to investigate universal religious wisdom by means of science.

Blavatsky claimed that her cosmology was based on her contact with a brotherhood of Himalayan masters whom she

*Helena Blavatsky, a co-founder and prominent personality of the Theosophical Society.*

*Henry Steel Olcott, co-founder of the Theosophical Society.*

*Annie Besant, a leading Theosophist and a supporter of rights for women, as a young woman, c.1868.*

*Madame Blavatsky with the emblem of the Theosophical Society above her head. At the centre of the emblem is the six-pointed star of the Seal of Solomon, a sign of the macro-cosm, surmounted by a crowned swastica, symbol of light and life, and surrounded by an ouroboros, a snake biting its own tail and representing cyclicity. The Egyptian ankh to the left symbolizes life, while the square topped by a triangle represents human beings: the triangle signifies the spiritual element, while the square portrays the material dimension.*

called the "Great White Brotherhood". The masters formed a "cosmic radio" to link humans with the chiefs of the divine hierarchy, which ruled the cosmos.

Blavatsky published *The Secret Doctrine* in 1888 and sought to explain universal creation as a scheme by which the primal unity of an unmanifest divine being filtered down into consciously evolving beings. The spirit was attempting, through a series of rebirths and by moving through the cosmos from planet to planet, to recover from a fall from divine grace. According to Blavatsky's view, a lord of the world originally came from Venus with several helpers who were, in descending order of authority:

Buddha; Mahachshan; Manu (who had an assistant Master Morya or "M"); and Maitreya (who had an assistant Master Koot Hoomi or "KH"). The two assistants Master Morya and Master Koot Hoomi were Blavatsky's masters and probably played a vital role in the founding of the Theosophical Society.

In 1909 a leading Theosophist Charles Leadbeater "discovered" a young Indian boy named Jiddu Krishnamurti, who he thought to be the avatar – the incarnation of divine consciousness on earth – of Maitreya, and the new Messiah and World Teacher. Annie Besant, a leading free-thinker, advocate of women's rights and

a socialist, took a maternal charge of Krishnamurti. Eventually turning away from Theosophy, Krishnamurti developed his own spiritual teachings on finding truth within and liberation from organized religion.

The Theosophical Society has had a major influence on modern Western magic, particularly on Samuel Liddell "MacGregor" Mathers and William Westcott, who were founders of the Hermetic Order of the Golden Dawn. The Society was also responsible for introducing Eastern ideas about reincarnation to Western occultism.

*Annie Besant with Krishnamurti, the Theosophical Society's chosen World Leader, who later disassociated himself from the organization.*

## THE GOLDEN DAWN

The creation of the magical society called the Hermetic Order of the Golden Dawn in the late nineteenth century marked an important milestone in the history of Western magic. It was primarily a synthesis of a number of occult traditions, and brought the mystical union with the divine to the forefront of modern magic by combining Hermeticism (which suggested that divine powers are latent within human beings, who may recover them by learning their own true natures) with a study of cabbala (through which humans can achieve union with God by the study of the Tree of Life).

The Golden Dawn resembled the Societas Rosicruciana and Freemasonry with its structure of initiations, elaborate ceremonies and use of occult symbolism. Like theosophy it offered leading roles to women, and a number of well-known women played a leading part – such as the actress Florence Farr, the Irish nationalist Maud Gonne, Moina Bergson, sister of the philosopher Henri Bergson, and wife of the founding member Samuel "MacGregor" Mathers, and Annie Horniman, the tea heiress. The society also attracted the eminent Irish poet William Butler Yeats, who had joined the Theosophical Society as an art student in the 1880s.

### THE FOUNDING MEMBERS

The Hermetic Order of the Golden Dawn was founded in London in 1888 by three members of the Societas Rosicruciana in Anglia, a Masonic-Rosicrucian body formed by Robert Wentworth Little in 1865 and based on the Rosicrucian legend of Christian Rosencreutz. They were called William Wynn Westcott (1848–1915), a doctor, coroner, Mason and

*Left: The Irish nationalist Maud Gonne, a member of the Golden Dawn.*

*William Butler Yeats, the Irish poet, dramatist and member of the Hermetic Order of the Golden Dawn.*

*Above: Annie Horniman inherited a large fortune from her father's tea business; she was a theatre manager and founder of the repertory system, as well as a member of the Golden Dawn.*

member of the Theosophical Society, William Robert Woodman (1828–91), a doctor, Mason, cabbala enthusiast and Supreme Magus of the Societas Rosicruciana, and Samuel Liddell "MacGregor" Mathers (1854–1918), a Mason who "spent almost half a lifetime in the British Museum in London and the Arsenal library in Paris, delving into magical and alchemical texts". Mathers, a particularly colourful and flamboyant character who assumed the title of Count MacGregor of Glenstrae, was

*Dr William Wynn Westcott, co-founder along with Samuel Mathers and William Woodman of the Hermetic Order of the Golden Dawn.*

*Samuel Liddell "MacGregor" Mathers was mainly responsible for bringing together various magical systems into the Hermetic Order of the Golden Dawn. A lover of ceremony, he is here shown performing the Rites of Isis.*

responsible for constructing a coherent magical system from the various elements of Masonic symbolism, cabbala, tarot, astrology, numerology and ritual magic. A fourth founder member, who died soon after the establishment of the Order, was the Rev. A. F. A. Woodford, a country vicar, who had acquired some manuscripts in cypher from the mystic and would-be magician Fred Hockley. He sent them to Westcott to decode and they proved to be a skeletal

description, in English, of five hitherto unknown rituals of a Rosicrucian nature which the writer had witnessed – presumably in Germany, as the manuscript also contained the address of a certain Anna Sprengel of Nuremburg, allegedly a high-grade Rosicrucian. Westcott asked Mathers for his co-operation in working up the bare bones of the system into a coherent whole suitable for "lodge-work", and to this Mathers agreed.

## EARLY SPIRITUAL LINKS

In October 1887 Westcott wrote to Fraulein Sprengel asking for occult teaching. This was given in a correspondence course and honorary grades were conferred upon Westcott, Mathers and Woodman. A charter was given for the establishment of a Golden Dawn Temple to work the grades in the cypher manuscript. Temples were set up in London, Weston-super-Mare, Bradford, Edinburgh and Paris. In 1891 the correspondence with Anna Sprengel stopped: a communication from Germany informed Westcott that his correspondent was dead and that no further information would be given to the English students; if they wished to establish a link with the Secret Chiefs of the Order they must do it themselves.

Mathers and Westcott were both friends of Madame Blavatsky and, while she lived, there was a friendly alliance between the Theosophical Society and the Golden Dawn. The roots of the two societies are deeply intertwined and the two organizations saw themselves as an élite, secretly working towards humanity's evolution. In 1892 Blavatsky died; Mathers claimed to have established links with the Secret Chiefs and supplied rituals for a Golden Dawn Second Order: the Red Rose and the Cross of Gold, based on the legend of Christian Rosencreutz. These rituals were adopted and a "Vault of the Adepts" became the controlling force behind the Temples of the Golden Dawn in the Order.

Mathers based his system on Eliphas Lévi's system of magic, which itself drew on Mesmer's theories that the planets influenced human beings

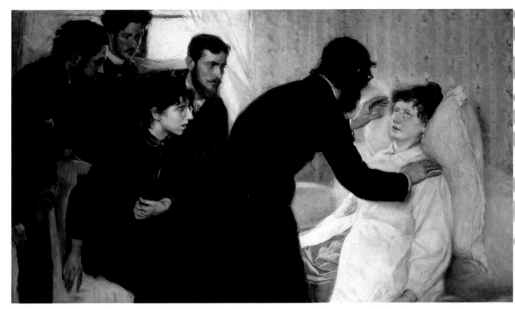

*Mesmer's theories of magnetism, as a universal fluid that could be controlled by human will, were extremely popular in the nineteenth century. Here a physician attempts a cure through hypnotism.*

through the fluid of animal magnetism. Mesmer claimed to have discovered that animal magnetism, as a universal medium, could be directly controlled by the human will. This became a basis of modern magical theory.

Lévi identified animal magnetism as the "astral light", which, like a magnet, had opposite poles that carried good and evil, and responded to the human will.

He said, "To direct the magnetic forces is then to destroy or create forms; to produce all appearance, or to destroy bodies; it is to exercise the mighty powers of Nature".

### Organized Magic

Eclectic in nature, the Golden Dawn used many deity forms including Hebrew, Christian and classical, and

# Symbols of the Hermetic Order of the Golden Dawn

Samuel "MacGregor" Mathers, a co-founder of the Golden Dawn, was fond of saying "There is no part of me that is not of the Gods". He paraphrased this from the Book of the Dead. Mathers and other Golden Dawn members used god forms from various cultures as currents or potencies of energies, which could be tapped during ritual. These energies were embodied in the design of wands, banners and badges such as these.

*The Order of the Pectoral, with signs of the zodiac. The swastika, as an emblem of light and life, was a spiritual sign before it was adopted by the Nazis.*

*Pectoral Cross with Hebrew characters showing Judaeo-Christian influences, particularly through Rosicrucianism.*

*A symbol used in the Hermes Lodge of the Stella Matutina. The triangle represents the number three, symbolizing the highest realm of the spiritual world.*

these reflected the spiritual interests of its various members. Mathers declared, in true theosophical fashion, that the order respected the truths of all religions, and he created a flexible system of magic, which could be used in many different ways.

Mathers loved the ornate trappings and highly organized aspects of ceremonial magic, and he ran the Golden Dawn like a military organization. But in 1900 his imperious behaviour eventually caused a rebellion among the other members. Mathers had accused Westcott of forging the foundation documents, and the other members of the Golden Dawn claimed that Mathers had put the authority of the order under question. This infuriated Mathers who decided to curse them all; according to one account, he took a packet of dried peas, rattled them violently in a sieve, and called on the demonic forces of Beelzebub and Seth-Typhon to wreak vengeance on his opponents.

## REBELLIONS AND SCHISMS

Further disagreements splintered the Golden Dawn, and the poet William Butler Yeats took control of the rebel faction for a time. The Christian mystic A. E. Waite took command of the London temple. Born in Brooklyn, New York, Waite was brought up a Roman Catholic, but became interested in spiritualism and theosophy before he joined the Golden Dawn in 1891. He wrote a number of books and is perhaps best known for designing the most widely used modern tarot pack, illustrated by Pamela Coleman Smith.

The Golden Dawn eventually fragmented into four daughter organizations: the Isis-Urania Temple, a Christian mystical organization run by Waite and others; the Stella Matutina run by R. W. Felkin and J. W. Brodie-Innes; the Alpha et Omega run by Brodie-Innes and Mathers; and the pagan A.A. headed by Aleister Crowley.

*Aleister Crowley wearing a robe of the Golden Dawn. Note the Rosy Cross on his chest.*

*A "certificate" of initiation into the Golden Dawn showing that Allan Bennett, a disciple of Aleister Crowley, was initiated by Samuel Mathers.*

*Below: Samuel Mathers and Moina Mathers, his wife, dressed as priest and priestess.*

# ALEISTER CROWLEY

Aleister Crowley, a one-time member of the Golden Dawn, is perhaps the most notorious occultist of the twentieth century and is famous for being a "black magician". He is one of the few people whose reputation extends outside the world of magic and witchcraft. Crowley, the self-styled "beast", was a controversial figure and courted publicity of the worst kind, but he was a talented magician and his ideas about magic remain influential today. He developed a system of magical anarchism – his declared creed was: "Do what thou wilt shall be the whole of the law" – and his ideas have also shaped the development and organization of modern witchcraft.

*"The beast" – Aleister Crowley.*

Edward Alexander Crowley was brought up a strict member of the Plymouth Brethren, but he decided to rebel, and as he explains in his autohagiography, at the age of 12 years he "simply went over to Satan's side". Crowley eventually developed his own theology, which was based on personal communication with the Devil against the forces of good, which had "constantly oppressed" him. Thus, Crowley's magical work is a direct rebellion against Christianity.

## THE BOOK OF LAW

Crowley joined the Golden Dawn in 1898 after leaving Cambridge. In April 1904, Crowley "received" the Book of the Law from an intelligence named Aiwass, mediated through his clairvoyant wife Rose Kelly. From this he developed the religion of Thelema. Thelema (which means "the will" in Greek) was said by Crowley to represent a new aeon, which would release humankind from its obsession with fear and its consciousness of sin. Crowley's brand of magic was based on Lévi's theories, which made the human being the centre of the universe. Lévi's view of magic emphasized finding the "True Will", which is the magician's magical identity – his or her "true self". Drawing on these ideas, Crowley claimed that each individual should be the centre of his or her own universe.

Aleister Crowley's writing on magic is widely regarded by magicians as

brilliant; his excessive, publicity-seeking behaviour, on the other hand, is often deplored (except by his direct followers, the Thelemites) as giving magic a "bad name". In Crowley's scheme of things, the knowledge of the will is the basis of a magician's empowerment, and the evolution of what he termed the Aeon of Horus is the aeon of individualism. Crowley's aim was the emancipation of humankind by the announcement of an "unconditional truth", which was "appropriate for the present evolutionary stage". This truth was to create an interpretation of the cosmos from an egocentric and practical viewpoint.

Thelema was a new cosmology and set of ethics for the Aeon of Horus. This marked a new stage evolving from the previous stage of the worship of the Father, which had followed on from the worship of the Mother. The Aeon of Horus was thus the aeon of the Child, which would, according to Crowley, destroy the Christian formula of the "Dying God" by offering complete moral independence, in this way releasing humankind from fear and the consequences of sin. Humanity was to govern itself, and self-sacrifice was viewed as

*Aleister Crowley in Golden Dawn robes.*

romantic folly. The sacrifice of the strong to the weak was, according to this view, against the principles of evolution.

## Do What Thou Wilt

From these ideas Crowley developed the maxim: "Do what thou wilt shall be the whole of the law", meaning that every person had the right to fulfil their own will and in so doing had the forces of the universe behind them. He defined the magician as one who knows the "Science and Art of causing Change to occur in conformity with Will". He believed that magic was the science of understanding the self and its conditions, and was the art of putting that knowledge into practical action.

Thus Crowley's religion of Thelema was based on the idea that the individual was a star within its own galaxy. "In a galaxy each star has its own magnitude, characteristics and direction, and the celestial harmony is best maintained by its attending to its own business."

*A self-portrait. Note that the medal around his neck is inscribed 666, denoting the beast from the Book of Revelations in the Christian Bible.*

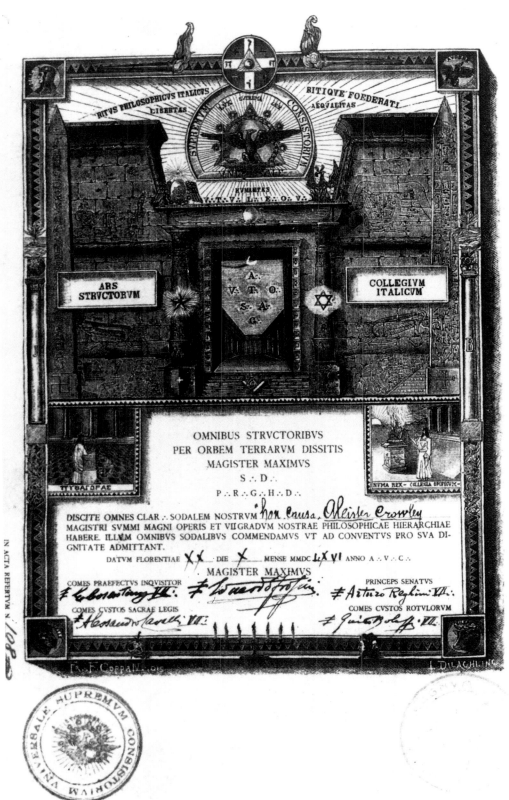

*The certificate acknowledging Aleister Crowley as a member of the High Order of the Freemasons of the 33rd Rite in Scotland.*

Crowley's version of magic puts the magician as a human being in control of his or her will firmly at the centre of magical practices and thus in control of the universe; this creates a sharp break from ideas of theosophical spiritual evolutionism and the Christian notion of union with God as expounded by some members of the Hermetic Order of the Golden Dawn.

## LIBERATION PHILOSOPHY

Aleister Crowley was a controversial figure, but there is no doubt that he was extremely influential in the shaping of modern magic. Crowley's major philosophical influence was through a liberation philosophy that focused on recreating a powerful magical self, and his impact stemmed from his connection of themes of human evolution (the Aeon of Horus) with modernism (the development of the self through the will). He is also identified as playing a part in the creation of modern witchcraft as a nature religion, although how much he actually contributed is contested. His poem, *Hymn to Pan*, written in 1929, displays classical themes combined with a focus on nature:

*Thrill with the lissome lust of the light,*
*O man! My man!*
*Come careering out of the night*
*Of Pan! Io Pan!*
*Io Pan! Io Pan! Come over the sea*
*From Sicily and from Arcady!*
*Roaming as Bacchus, with fauns and pards*
*And nymphs and satyrs for thy guards,*
*On a milk-white ass, come over the sea*
*To me, to me,*
*Come with Apollo in bridal dress*
*(Shepherdess and pythoness)*
*Come with Artemis, silken shod,*
*And wash thy white thigh, beautiful God,*
*In the moon of the woods, on the*
*marble mount,*
*The dimpled dawn of the amber fount!*
*Dip the purple of passionate prayer*
*In the crimson shrine, the scarlet snare,*
*The soul that startles in eyes of blue*
*To watch thy wantoness weeping through*
*The tangled grove, the gnarl'd bole*
*Of the living tree that is spirit and soul*
*And body and brain – come over the sea,*
*(Io Pan! Io Pan!)*
*Devil or god, to me, to me,*
*My man! My man! ...*

## ORDO TEMPLI ORIENTIS

Crowley was influenced by Eastern schools of thought such as Buddhism and Tantrism, and joined the Ordo Templi Orientis in 1912, becoming its leader in 1922. The Ordo Templi Orientis (OTO) had been founded at the beginning of the twentieth century

*Aleister Crowley towards the end of his life.*

*A card from the tarot deck designed by Crowley and painted by Frieda Harris in 1941.*

by Karl Kellner, a German Mason and occultist. It is claimed that it was the product of the German occult revival, which was sparked off by the opening of the Berlin branch of the Theosophical Society in 1884. The OTO was a modern form of Templarism, drawing on the Knights Templar movement, which had been suppressed in the fourteenth century on the grounds of heresy, sodomy and bestiality. Kellner is said to have been initiated into the use of "the sexual current" by an Arab called Soliman ben Aifa and two Indian Tantrics, Bhima Sen Pratap and Shri Mahatma Agamya Paramahamsa. He was also influenced by a group of French followers of the American occultist P. B. Randolph. The OTO made grand claims that it possessed the key that would open up all Masonic and Hermetic secrets through the teaching of sexual magic. Reuss invited Crowley to rewrite the OTO rituals, and it has been suggested that Crowley saw the OTO as the first great

*"The Resurrection of Zoroaster", a drawing by Austin Osman Spare, 1905.*

*"Blood on the Moon" by Austin Osman Spare, 1955.*

magical order to accept the Law of Thelema, and by doing so to slough off the techniques of ceremonial magic and to revive pagan elements of ecstasy and wonder as the keys to the "Mysteries of Man".

### AUSTIN OSMAN SPARE (1886–1956)

Austin Osman Spare was a pupil of Crowley, and he was also the protégé of a Mrs Patterson, who was said to be a hereditary witch descended from a line of witches from Salem, Massachusetts. Spare developed a method of "atavistic resurgence" – the evocation of beings from the primitive depths of the mind, which could make themselves known through visions and art. His magical philosophy was based on the power of

*A symbolic painting for Crowley's Temple of the A.A., the Order of the Silver Star.*

the will to influence the subconscious mind, and he believed that it was possible to instruct the subconscious mind through the creation of personal symbols known as sigils. A sigil could be implanted into the unconscious by making the mind blank at the time of a magical act, at sexual orgasm, or through self-hypnosis. Spare's "Cult of the Zos and the Kia" – or Zos Kia Cultus – was informed by his contact with Mrs Patterson and was based on the idea that it was possible to retrace earlier existences. After locating the first personality (Zos) it could be transcended and merged with the void (which he called Kia) through sexual union. Spare's magical ideas have formed an important part of chaos magic practice. Chaos magic is the ultimate expression of liberation philosophy in magical practices.

# DION FORTUNE

Considered one of the leading occultists of her time, Dion Fortune was perhaps one of the first occult writers to approach magic and Hermetic concepts using the precepts of psychology, in particular of Jung and Freud. Her role was a significant one and the written material she left behind is still used today, valued in particular for its rich source for rituals, and its pagan themes. Dion Fortune also succeeded in bringing about a renewal of interest in British myths and legends, and their importance in the country's historical inheritance. She was also instrumental in emphasizing the importance of balance between male and female elements in magic.

*A rare photograph of the young Dion Fortune. The picture was taken in 1911, at the beginning of her studies at Warwick Horticultural College.*

Dion Fortune was born Violet Mary Firth on 6 December 1890 to a wealthy family in the steel business. She adapted the family motto, "Deo, non Fortuna", to create her magical name. A leading magician of her time, Dion Fortune had been initiated into the Hermetic Order of the Golden Dawn in 1919 but, according to her biographer Alan Richardson, she disliked the idea of pouring the "regenerative spiritual force of the East into the group-soul of the British Empire". Being a staunch British nationalist, Dion Fortune also reacted against the Eastern influence in theosophy and turned instead to a mystical Christianity and what she saw as the indigenous British mythology of King Arthur and the Holy Grail.

Acting on these convictions, in 1923 she formed a Christian Mystic Lodge of the Theosophical Society with the aim of interpreting Christianity in terms of theosophy and vice versa, but she eventually rejected the ideas of the Theosophical Society in 1928 and went on to develop her own magical society.

A pupil of the occultist Theodore Moriarty, who taught that the "Christ Principle" had first been propounded in Atlantis and was manifested through Horus, Mithras, Quetzalcoatl and Buddha, Dion Fortune began to form her own magical contacts. During the winter of 1923–4 she contacted the people she referred to as her secret chiefs, and in 1927 she left the Hermetic Order of the Golden Dawn to found the Fraternity of the Inner Light (still in existence today as the Society of the Inner Light).

Dion Fortune's secret chiefs included a trinity of masters, with Melchisedec of Salem as the source. These three chiefs sent out three distinct "rays" of wisdom, which were defined as the following: the Hermetic Ray, which was concerned with philosophy and ritual; the Orphic or Green Ray, which was devoted to earth mysteries; and the Mystic Ray, which was concerned with the mysteries of the Son. From 1926 Dion Fortune published a number of books on magical

*For Dion Fortune the Knights of the Round Table represented a chivalric era that could be magically tapped into.*

*The death of King Arthur and his passage to another plane was central to his mystic significance.*

cosmology, cabbala and practical magic, as well as many novels with an occult theme. The most famous of her novels was *The Sea Priestess*, first published in 1938.

## THE INFLUENCE OF CARL JUNG

Carl Gustav Jung created an individual practice of spiritual rebirth, and he has been called a prophet by spiritual seekers; it has also been claimed that Jungian psychology has helped to legitimize modern paganism, and indeed his psychology has had a major influence on modern magic, primarily through the work of Dion Fortune. Carl Gustav Jung was the founder of analytical psychology. His methods included using the active imagination and amplifying dream and fantasy images; he thought that people from every society were predisposed to form what he called archetypal images – certain symbols that were found cross-culturally in mythology, fairy tales and religious iconography. During the period 1914–18 Jung experienced a psychological breakdown, and for the rest of his life he sought explanations for what had

*The ideas of Swiss psychologist Carl Gustav Jung had a profound influence on the magical work of Dion Fortune.*

happened to him, trying to understand the images and symbols that had arisen from his unconscious. Jung attempted to liberate the unconscious and developed what has since turned out to be a form of spiritual cult based on trying to understand the mystical process of "inner reality", which will hopefully produce a new secret wisdom. Jung took the idea of the unconscious seriously and developed techniques for encouraging dissociation – freeing the mind from its usual patterns of conscious thought – so that the unconscious could regulate actions.

Much of Carl Jung's theory stemmed from a powerful dream that he once had of a house with a number of floors: he took the upper storey to represent his consciousness and the ground floor to symbolize his unconsciousness. From the ground floor was a stairway leading down to a cellar; the cellar led in turn down to a cave. This is how he described the dream:

*I was in a house I did not know, which had two storeys. It was "my house". I found myself in the upper storey where there was a kind of salon furnished with fine pieces in rococo style ... It occurred to me that I did not know what the lower floor looked like. Descending the stairs, I reached the ground floor. There everything was much older ... The furnishings were medieval; the floors were of red brick. Everywhere it was rather dark ... Beyond it, I discovered a stone stairway that led down into the cellar. Descending again, I found myself in a beautifully vaulted room, which looked exceedingly ancient ... I knew that the walls dated from Roman times ... I looked more closely at the floor. It was of stone slabs, and in one of these I discovered a ring. When I pulled it, the stone slab lifted, again I saw a stairway of narrow stone steps leading down into the depths ... I descended, and entered a low cave cut into the rock. Thick dust lay on the floor, and in the dust were scattered bones*

*Much of Dion Fortune's work focused on the magical power of the Goddess as the feminine aspect of a cosmic polarity. Isis, characterized as the sea priestess in one of her novels, was especially important.*

*and broken pottery, like the remains of a primitve culture. I discovered two human skulls, obviously very old and half disintegrated. Then I awoke.*

Interpreting this house as an image of his psyche, Jung saw his consciousness as represented by the salon; the ground floor as his first level of unconsciousness; the cave represented the world of the primitive human within himself, an area that he thought was scarcely reached by consciousness.

Jung's main theme was of the evolution of consciousness. The first stage of this process was through contacting the "world of memories", which led to a rebirth through the realm of the underworld, the ancestors and the dead. He said that his psychoanalytic techniques were like an archaeological excavation and involved using the active imagination to contact the ancestral past.

The unconscious, for Jung, consisted of all the forgotten material from an individual's own past and the inherited behavioural traces of the "human spirit". Contact with what he called the "collective unconscious" – symbolized by gods – led to access to wisdom and universal human experience. Jung also developed notions of what he called the animus and the anima. The animus was

the masculine aspect of a woman's psyche, while the anima was the corresponding feminine part of a man's psyche. His psychology put much emphasis on integrating the contra-sexual other. In other words, a woman must get in touch with her "masculine" psychic self and a man his "feminine" to achieve psychic harmony.

## THE HARMONIOUS UNION

In her magical novels, Dion Fortune utilizes Jung's notions of animus and anima as masculine and feminine forces, whereby a woman develops her masculinity and a man his femininity.

In *The Sea Priestess*, sea priestesses and priests came from the mythical island of Atlantis – which was for Fortune, as for many occultists, the home of divine wisdom – and engaged in selective breeding rites to pass on magical lore. The work focused on the magical power of the Goddess, as the feminine part of a polarity underpinning the cosmos, and, according to the historian Ronald Hutton, drew on three influences: her reading of D. H. Lawrence; her husband Thomas Penry Evans' interest in the god Pan; and the interest shown in the

*Dion Fortune pictured with her husband on the left, and an unknown friend on the right.*

Great Mother and women's mysteries by Charles Seymour, her magical partner. As Isis, goddess of nature and the fertility of the land, the sea priestess draws her partner, the Lord of the Sun, into magical union:

*Isis of Nature awaiteth the coming of her Lord the Sun. She calls him. She draws him from the place of the dead, the Kingdom of Amenti, where all things are forgotten. And he comes to her in his boat called Millions of Years, and the earth grows green with the springing grain. For the desire of Osiris answereth unto the call of Isis. And so it will ever be in the hearts of men, for thus the gods have formed them.*

At the beginning of World War Two, Dion Fortune became involved in a number of magical operations against Germany. Seeing Britain as being under threat from the forces of evil, she organized a magical meditation group from the Society of the Inner Light to confront the evils of Hitler's Nazi forces. Fortune wrote weekly letters to her students between 1939 and 1942, and every Sunday morning from 12.15 until 12.30 members were asked to meditate on the forces of good overcoming evil.

## FORTUNE'S LEGACY

Dion Fortune's work has greatly influenced modern magic, especially the practices, rituals and ceremonies of witchcraft, which is focused on the Goddess. Her ideas and the words she wrote have influenced many different aspects of magic, and she is respected by diverse groups of people.

Dion Fortune's work has also brought a renewed focus on British mythology – especially that of King Arthur – that has revitalized links with historical traditions, and she has also helped to bring about an emphasis on the spiritual harmony of balancing feminine and masculine aspects of the psyche in magical practice.

*Inside the Temple of the Grail by W. Hauschild. The Grail represented a source of spiritual wisdom for Dion Fortune.*

*Dion Fortune and her Society of the Inner Light fought a spiritual Battle of Britain to protect the country from invasion by Hitler's forces.*

# WITCHCRAFT TODAY

Modern witchcraft, or Wicca as it is also known, is a form of spirituality that seeks harmony with nature. Usually celebrating eight seasonal festivals, witches honour nature – both within their bodies, which are seen as sacred, and in the wider environment. Combining a positive view of women and an ecological awareness, this new form of religion seeks a holistic way of experiencing and understanding the world. This modern definition of witchcraft is very different to that of the early modern era, when witches were viewed as evil by the Christian Church. This chapter examines the different strands of witchcraft that are practised today, and highlights the various influences and personalities involved in the movement.

# TODAY'S WITCHES

Modern witchcraft is a far cry from the witchcraft imagined and created by the Christian Church during the witch hunts of the early modern period in Europe. Rather than being in league with the Devil and practising evil acts, today's witches are seeking a relationship with nature and the changing seasons of the natural world, experienced within themselves as an intuitive understanding. Reclaiming the word "witch", not as an anti-social person who is seen to have magical and malign powers, but rather to describe the cunning woman or man living within a community, they attune themselves with the powers of nature. All of nature – the land, mountains, lakes – as well as the past, as seen through ancient cultures, is viewed as sacred.

*Modern witches relate to what they see as a time when people were more in contact with nature and the natural environment. Here, at Trethevey in Cornwall, England, offerings have been left near prehistoric rock carvings.*

The witchcraft that is becoming increasingly popular today is not the witchcraft practised in small indigenous societies around the world, nor the diabolic type of witchcraft imagined by the Christian church during the European witch hunts. It is a witchcraft that is a form of spirituality: modern witchcraft is a religious practice that venerates nature. It was created in the 1950s using the structure of Western high magic ritual to worship the natural forces inherent in nature personified as various gods and goddesses. This form of witchcraft is not part of an ancient pre-Christian paganism, but instead draws on many sources from the Western magic tradition as well as some of the craft magic of the country cunning folk.

Modern witchcraft is gaining many new members who are disenchanted with mainstream religions, which are increasingly seen by many as being out of touch with direct spiritual experience. People are also attracted to witchcraft because it views women and sexuality as sacred, and this marks an important distinction between this new form of religion and more orthodox faiths, which frequently hold that women are in some ways inferior or less spiritual than men.

Another reason for its appeal is that as ecological awareness increases, modern witchcraft, as part of a wider group of pagan practices, offers a spirituality which is in tune with the natural world – it seeks harmony with nature, rather than its domination or control.

Witchcraft is just one spiritual path within a group of magical practices

*A modern witches' altar showing a pentacle, a five-sided star symbolic of the union of the five senses of the human body – sight, hearing, smell, taste and touch – and of the four elements – fire, air, earth and water – and of the spirit.*

commonly referred to as paganism. The term "pagan" comes from the Latin *paganus*, meaning "rustic", and was first used to distinguish unfavourably those who did not belong to the dominant urban faith of Christianity. More recently, historians have debated the origins of the word, and it has been suggested that it originally referred to non-military civilians – those not enrolled in the army of God. Another suggestion was that the word *pagani* was used to designate followers of an older religion when the earlier, non-military meaning had ceased to have relevance. However, by the end of the nineteenth century, "pagan" had a clear association with the countryside and the natural world, and this is largely because of its association with the Romantic movement.

Romanticism was one of a range of alternative political visions in the nineteenth century. Drawing on Renaissance theories of the connections or correspondences between the material world and the creative imagination, nature was seen as visible spirit; Romanticism involved a heightened sensitivity to the natural world. The Romantic movement was a reaction against the Enlightenment's celebration of reason, progress and notions of a common humanity and universal truth. By contrast, Romanticism valued the individual, the relative and the internal; it explored different levels of consciousness, the supernatural and mythic interpretations of the world. Wild woods, once seen as a threat to the forces of civilization, now offered the opportunity of solitude, contemplation and oneness with nature. The experience of nature became a spiritual act: nature was not only beautiful, but was uplifting and morally healing. This was particularly well expressed in the works of poets such as Wordsworth, Coleridge, Blake, Byron and Keats.

Inspired by the spirit of the Romantic movement and by his knowledge of Western magic and folklore, Gerald Gardner, the founder of the modern witchcraft movement, crafted a new religion based on the creation of a sacred ceremonial circle in which gods,

*The land is imbued with history and mythology as here in Cornwall, England, where the Inner Ward of Tintagel Castle, the legendary birth place of King Arthur, may be seen above the wizard Merlin's Cave.*

goddesses and the spirits of nature could be invoked. This religion of witchcraft would come to take a prominent place in the spiritual and cultural history of Western Europe, the United States, Australia and other parts of the world.

Modern witchcraft is a new religion – its roots cannot be traced back to an ancient pre-Christian pagan tradition. It draws its inspiration from the past, and although often archaeologically and historically inaccurate in its claims, it nevertheless is in tune with a different, more holistic way of understanding the world, one that would probably have been understood by our ancestors.

*The traditional European view of natural springs as sacred places survives today at "clootie wells", where rags are tied to nearby trees as offerings to the spirit of the place.*

# GERALD GARDNER

The founder of modern witchcraft, Gerald Gardner claimed that he had been initiated into a witch coven in the New Forest, England, in 1939, by a woman named "Old Dorothy". Whether this is true or not remains unclear. However, Gardner was deeply influenced by the work of Margaret Murray who stated that the victims of the early modern witch hunts were practitioners of a surviving paganism which she described as the "Old Religion". Murray's ideas have since been disproved – modern witchcraft is not a form of the ancient paganism practised in pre-Christian times – but her influence on the birth of a new religion created by Gardner is enormous. In 1951, the repeal of the Witchcraft and Vagrancy Acts provided Gardner with the opportunity of promoting and publicizing his witch religion.

*A late photograph of the highly creative Gerald Gardner, thought by many people to be the founder of modern witchcraft.*

The form that modern witchcraft has taken is largely due to the imagination and creative flair of Gerald Gardner (1884–1964). He united paganism with the figure of the witch; he was what the historian Ronald Hutton calls the originator of a countercultural religion based on a nature goddess and a horned god. Gardner argued that witchcraft was an ancient, pre-Christian, pagan mystery tradition.

## THE BEGINNINGS

Gardner had a keen interest in magic and at various times in his life was involved in Freemasonry, spiritualism, Buddhism and other, magical practices. He put many magical ideas and practices in his book *Witchcraft Today*. It was published in 1954, after the repeal of the laws against witchcraft in Britain, and it became the foundation text of modern witchcraft. Gardner was helped by his friend Ross Nichols (then leader of the Ancient Druid Order, and later the founder of the Order of Bards, Ovates and Druids) in the creation of a series of rituals, that were conducted within a purified circle, and the aim of which was to contain and channel the magical powers released from the participants' bodies.

At one time an owner/manager of tea and rubber plantations in Ceylon, North Borneo and Malaya, Gardner later became an inspector in the Malay customs service. He retired to London in 1936 at the age of 52, then moved to the New Forest in 1938. It was there that he joined the Rosicrucian Theatre in Christchurch, and was, so he says, initiated into a surviving coven by a mysterious woman

*A modern witchcraft Yule altar with decorations that represent the seasonal festival.*

named "Old Dorothy". He worked with this coven until the late 1940s, forming a magical partnership with a woman called "Dafo". In 1947 they created a company to buy a plot of land near a naturist club in St Albans in Hertfordshire, England, and there erected a reconstruction of a sixteenth-century witch's cottage. This cottage, which had cabbalistic symbols painted on the inside, provided the focus for a working coven, which was run by Gerald Gardner and Dafo in the early 1950s.

## MARGARET MURRAY

Gardner was greatly influenced by the Egyptologist Margaret Murray. In 1921 she had published a book called *The Witch-Cult in Western Europe* in which she stated that the victims of the early modern witch hunts were practitioners of a surviving pagan religion. Murray claimed that an incarnate deity, in the form of a god, had been worshipped but that this may have been because the god superseded the Mother Goddess; she said that the position of the chief woman was obscure, but that the worship of a female deity had probably been supplanted by that of the male. The witchcraft rites varied with the seasons, but "The greater number of the ceremonies appear to have been practised for the purpose of securing fertility", and a marriage took place, usually once a year.

In her autobiography, Murray describes how ancient religion was her pet subject and that during World War I she researched witchcraft as she was prevented from working in Egypt. She explains how she started:

"I started with the usual idea that witches were all old women suffering from illusions about the Devil and that their persecutors were wickedly prejudiced and perjured. I worked only from contemporary records, and when I suddenly realised that the so-called Devil was simply a disguised man I was startled, almost alarmed, by the way the recorded facts fell into place, and showed that the witches were members of an old, primitive form of religion and the records had been made by members of a new and persecuting form."

*A modern representation of a wicker man, a contemporary link with supposed pagan celebrations of the past.*

Giving the impression that there was a fairly uniform surviving pagan religion in Western Europe, Murray's work focused on the notion that witchcraft centred on fertility. The horned god represented the generative powers of nature and was personified by a male

*A portrait of Margaret Murray, Egyptologist and influential anthropologist.*

person during coven rituals. Sabbaths were held four times a year at All Hallows, Candlemas, May Day and Lammas during which there was much feasting, sacrifice of animals and children, processional dances and ritualized sexual intercourse to promote fertility. Homage was paid to the horned god.

Murray even claimed that Joan of Arc and her contemporary, Gilles de Rais, had been members of this ancient pre-Christian religion. In fact Murray had constructed this pre-Christian pagan religion, and simply ignored evidence that did not support her view. She wrote a second book, which was titled *The God of the Witches*, in 1933. In this, she celebrated what she described as the "Old Religion" and linked in folk tales and customs.

## GARDNER'S PRACTICAL MAGIC

The historian Ronald Hutton points out four lines of influence on Murray: first, Jules Michelet's *La Sorcière* (1862), which portrayed the pagan witch religion led by women as democratic and nature-loving. (Michelet also claimed

*The god Pan is thought to be a manifestation of the ancient horned god in modern witchcraft, largely because of the work of the Egyptologist, Margaret Murray.*

that the Renaissance had been caused by the natural wisdom of the witch religion working its way upwards to artists and writers). Second, Charles Godfrey Leland's *Aradia* (1899), which was directly inspired by Michelet and which purported to be the gospel of the Italian branch of Michelet's witch religion. Third, James Frazer's theory of evolution, which suggested that surviving folk customs could be the fossils of old religions. Finally, Murray's association with the Folklore Society. It was Murray's work that gave Gardner the idea of a fertility religion, but how did he put together a practical system for working magic?

Aidan Kelly has made a detailed study of modern witchcraft using his experience of studying the origins of Christianity as a historical problem. He could not discover any "ancient" material in Gerald Gardner's *Book of Shadows* (part of the witch's magical paraphernalia in which ritual details are recorded), and claims that the only magic that Gardner could find out about was high magic, which was inherently Judaeo-Christian and "too complex". Folk magic was too practical for Gardner's purposes:

methods of curing warts, or a knowledge of herbs and charms, do not offer a system or theological structure for working magic, so Gardner had to incorporate elements of high magic. Ronald Hutton says that there are four direct links between ancient paganism and Wicca, or modern witchcraft, and these are: high magic; the knowledge of the use of plants and herbs and spells; folk rites and customs to honour or manipulate the powers of nature; and finally, the literature and art of the ancient world. If Wicca is seen as a form of ritual magic – rather than an age-old paganism – then it has a distinguished and very long pedigree.

## CROWLEY'S INFLUENCE

As an initiate of Aleister Crowley's Ordo Templi Orientis (OTO), Gardner was also deeply influenced by Crowley's ideas and, according to one view, hired him to write witchcraft rituals for him. One version of events claims that Crowley was pleased to do this because he saw witchcraft as a "popularized form of his own creed". However, Ronald Hutton claims that there is no evidence for this and points to the fact that Aleister Crowley's writings about witchcraft were brief.

*A Secret Wicca ritual that is based on the work of Gardner, with the dramatic addition of lights and theatrical effects.*

The historian Gordon Melton claims that Gardner was influenced by high magic as described in Crowley's *Magick* (1929) and *The Book of the Law* (1936). Hutton argues that Gardner was initiated into all the degrees of the OTO and, in addition, that he was held to be Crowley's heir as head of the OTO but that he could not find enough people interested in joining it. Hutton further argues that Gardner had sympathies for both high magic and medieval witchcraft (through a reading of Margaret Murray) and that he "crossed the line" from one to the other, finally devoting himself to witchcraft. From 1947 to 1953 he was writing and devising rituals, which were either copied from existing rituals or were newly created.

## VENERATION OF THE GODDESS

Modern witchcraft is a religion that venerates women, the earth, the dark and nature, all of which have been denigrated by Christianity and by Western cultures generally. In *Witchcraft Today*, Gardner links death and rebirth with the myth of the Goddess. When the Goddess journeyed to the nether lands to solve all mysteries she encountered Death:

*The guardians of the portals challenged her: "Strip off thy garments, lay aside thy jewels, for nought may ye bring with you into this our land." So she laid down her garments and her jewels and was bound as are all who enter the realms of Death, the mighty one. Such was her beauty that Death himself knelt and kissed her feet, saying: "Blessed be thy feet that have brought thee in these ways . . . " [Death] taught her all the mysteries, and they loved and were one; and he taught her all the magics. For there are three great events in the life of man – love, death and resurrection in the new body – and magic controls them all.*

The god of Death falls in love with the Goddess and teaches her that he provides rest and peace, and that if humans love they will be reborn among their loved ones at the same time and in the same place. The myth of the

Many other goddesses, as well as a Great Mother Goddess, are venerated. Some, such as Lilith, embody the dark and death as well as more obvious life-giving and nurturing qualities. Lilith, a hybrid bird-woman, was Adam's first wife, but she refused to lie beneath him, and, uttering the magical name of God, flew away to the wilderness where she gave birth to demons. God sent three angels to bring her back to Eden, but she refused to return. Lilith is perhaps the source of ideas about strix, striga, or striges, the owl-like creatures in classical and European folklore, and later the prototypes of the diabolical witch stereotype created and fostered by the established Christian Church.

## THE GOD

The partner of the Goddess is the God. He is sometimes called Cernunnos or Herne, but is more frequently referred to merely as the horned god. The historian Ronald Hutton argues that the cultural forces that brought the modern perception of a single goddess also

*An owl mask worn to invoke the goddess Lilith. Demonized by the Christian Church, Lilith is seen by many magicians as the first feminist.*

delivered a single god as her consort. He points out that before the nineteenth century many gods had a variety of associations and connections, such as Jupiter (ruler), Neptune (sea), Mercury (commerce, education, communication), Vulcan (industry), and Apollo (poetry, the natural world). For the Romantic movement the god Pan, personified as wild nature, overshadowed them all. He became a major theme in the work of Wordsworth, Keats and Shelley, and represented the English countryside. He later featured in the literary works of Robert Louis Stevenson and in Kenneth Grahame's classic children's story *The Wind in the Willows*.

Hutton observes that Pan became the expression of the natural world as sublime, mysterious, and awe-inspiring but also benevolent and comforting; this was in direct contrast to the industrial and urban environment, and represented a return to the lost innocence of a rural paganism. In witchcraft, Pan became characterized as the horned god, not least through Margaret Murray's work *The God of the Witches*, published in 1933, which was formative in shaping modern ideas about a nature god.

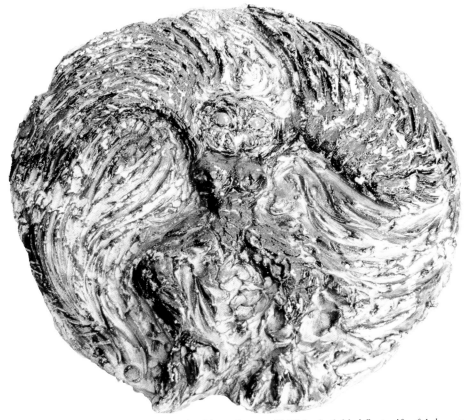

*A contemporary owl goddess plaque inspired by a dream of Lilith, the fabled first wife of Adam, who rejected him and his God, and fled from Eden.*

*Baubo, an ancient Greek figure who perched on a well making Demeter laugh when her daughter Persephone was in the Underworld. She represents the sacrality of women's bodies for many witches today.*

# CELEBRATING NATURE

Referred to as a "nature religion", modern witchcraft honours the Earth and the body rather than a transcendental spirit. The physical body and all of nature are seen as inherently divine and part of a larger whole, commonly seen to consist of interconnecting energies. Many modern witches take the view that their religion is the Old Religion of the village wise woman and cunning man, who practised herbalism and divining as part of their craft. Most now accept that there is no unbroken tradition that connects their current practices with those of the cunning folk, but modern witches talk about a sense of connectedness with nature, which links them spiritually and mythologically, if not historically, to a view of life where everything is connected through various energies and forces. Many are turning to direct action to protect the environment.

*A modern witch celebrates a Winter Solstice ritual in a forest.*

Witches today seek a relationship with nature, and conduct rituals to create a place where it is possible to be aware of the wider connecting pattern of the universe. This is often visualized as a web, a sacred force that is the very grounding of existence. Sometimes it is envisaged as a "web of wyrd", as outlined by the psychologist Brian Bates in his books *The Way of Wyrd* (1983) and *The Wisdom of Wyrd* (1996). Human beings are seen to be a part of nature, intimately connected via a web of forces and energies.

In *Witchcraft Today*, Gerald Gardner, the founder of modern witchcraft, said that whereas ceremonial magicians used a circle to keep demons at bay, the witches that he knew worked within a magical circle to contain the power generated from their bodies. He outlined four great festivals that the witches celebrated – November eve (Hallowe'en), February eve, May eve and August eve – which corresponded to the ancient Gaelic fire festivals of Samhain (1 November), Brigid (1 February), Bealteine or Beltene (1 May) and Lugnasadh (1 August). Gardner wrote that the festivals corresponding to midwinter and midsummer were both said to have been founded in honour of female deities, while the two winter ones were those in which the God took precedence (although "he is not superior, but merely her equal").

## MODERN RITUALS

Today witches create a circle as sacred space "between the worlds" into which the divine, usually personified as the Goddess and God, manifests. The witchcraft circle is always arranged according to the cardinal points of north, south, east and west. Each cardinal direction has certain attributes, which relate to the natural world. Thus the circle is usually ceremonially opened in the east because the east represents light, the first light of dawn and also

*All of nature is seen to be part of a pattern of the universe to modern witches; some visualize this as a "web of wyrd", others as a manifestation of the Goddess.*

the spring; it is symbolic of air, intellect and rational thought. The magical tool of the east is the athame (a ritual knife or dagger) or the sword. The south represents fire and the energy of the magical will, the summer, sun and heat. It is symbolized by the wand, a slender branch of wood. The west represents water, the emotions, rivers, oceans, streams and autumn; it is symbolized by the cup or chalice. The west flows and merges while the east separates and canalizes. The north represents the earth, mountains, valleys, winter and the body. The pentacle is its symbol: its five points represent the five senses of the human body and all the elements: earth, air, fire, water and spirit. In the centre of the circle stands a large cauldron representing transformation: of the raw into the cooked and, on the spiritual level, of changes of consciousness within the natural rhythms of nature.

Wicca operates a seasonal myth cycle whereby the processes of nature – conception, birth, maturation and death – are portrayed in dynamic interaction with the Goddess and the God as personifications of the forces and powers

*Witchcraft harnesses the power of the mind, using natural objects and visualization techniques.*

*Many Wiccan rituals are performed outside. Here two initiates are bound into a coven.*

of nature. Thus the inner self of the individual witch is linked in with the wider mythological cycle.

The Wiccans Janet and Stewart Farrar, in their book *Eight Sabbats for Witches* (1981), work with what have now become the eight standard seasonal rituals for many pagans: Yule or Winter Solstice (22 December), Imbolg (2 February), Spring Equinox (21 March), Bealtaine (30 April), Midsummer or Summer Solstice (22 June), Lughnasadh (31 July), Autumn Equinox (21 September) and Samhain (31 October).

The Farrars have adapted Gardner's ritual year to reflect what they call a solar theme and a natural-fertility theme. The Goddess does not undergo the experiences but presides over them; she is always there but changes her aspect, while the God dies and is reborn. The solar theme, which dominates the solstices and equinoxes, reflects the concept of a sacrificed and resurrected god: he dies and is reborn at the Winter Solstice, and at the Spring Equinox his waxing power impregnates Mother Earth; he reaches his prime at the Summer Solstice, then his waning powers lead through to the Autumn Equinox and his death and

*Creative visualizations may be conducted outside, in the midst of nature, for inspiration.*

rebirth at the Winter Solstice to complete the cycle. The natural-fertility theme involves the god of the waxing year, represented by the Oak King, and the god of the waning year, personified as the Holly King – both aspects of the horned god, a natural-fertility figure. According to the Farrars, they are light and dark aspects of each other and compete eternally for the favour of the Great Mother. At Yule the Holly King ends his reign and falls to the Oak King, while at Midsummer the Oak King is replaced by the Holly King.

### THE ENVIRONMENT

Increasingly modern witches are looking to ritual sites in nature, and ancient stone monuments, to contact the energies of their ancestors, those that practised the "Old Religion". These sites, which often date from the neolithic, are often viewed as places of female mysteries and the land itself is though of as the Goddess incarnate. Believed to be gateways into the otherworld, a "dreamtime" that enables witches to connect with an inner sacred place within, these places are the locations for healing, divination, and the conducting of life rites such as handfastings (weddings). A Wiccan high priestess, Vivianne Crowley has observed that Wicca has changed its focus from the early days. She says that Gerald Gardner's original stress was on witchcraft as a fertility religion but that a more recent portrayal of witchcraft is as an environmental movement. Crowley notes that Gardner made little mention of nature, being more interested in magical powers and the traditional image of the witch as caster of spells, and points out that it was Doreen Valiente, Gardner's high priestess, who recast the concept of fertility into one that included the mind and the soul. Valiente thought that there was a spiritual as well as a material fertility, and that human life was like a desert without it. Valiente talks not so much

*Stone circles are especially sacred to modern witches and other pagans as places where the Earth's energies are particularly potent.*

# Paganism

Nature is central to modern pagan experience, and Selena Fox, Wiccan high priestess and founder of Circle Sanctuary in the United States, describes this side of paganism:

I am Pagan. I am a part of the whole of Nature. The Rocks, the Animals, the Plants, the Elements, and the Stars are my relatives. Other humans are my sisters and brothers, whatever their races, colors, genders, sexual orientations, ages, nationalities, religions, lifestyles. Planet Earth is my home. I am a part of this large family of Nature, not the master of it. I have my own special part to play and I seek to discover and play that part to the best of my ability. I seek to live in harmony with others in the family of Nature, treating others with respect ...

I am Pagan. Nature Spirituality is my religion and my life's foundation. Nature is my spiritual teacher and holy book. I am part of Nature and

*Witchcraft, as a part of modern paganism, views all of nature as sacred.*

Nature is part of me. My understanding of Nature's inner mysteries grows as I journey on this spiritual path.

about literal fertility but about finding harmony with nature; she calls the star goddess the soul of nature.

According to Vivianne Crowley, Wicca has changed from a secret fertility cult to a more open movement, with nature high on its agenda. This marks a significant transition whereby Wicca moves out of the darkness of witchery to take the moral high ground of environmentalism. To be at one with nature in one's inner self is no longer enough: radical action to preserve nature is now important. While many witches are content to cast spells to help nature, others are becoming involved in direct action. So witchcraft encompasses many different practices but all are focused on nature, both within and without, rather than a transcendental spirit that is separate from the natural world.

*To pagans, Nature is a source of divinity and enchantment, thought to be inhabited by spirits or "the little people".*

# DOREEN VALIENTE

If Gerald Gardner was the founder and "father" of modern witchcraft, then Doreen Valiente surely is his female counterpart. It was she who carried on and expanded his work in formulating and defining this relatively new form of paganism. A modest, unassuming woman, she brought a down-to-earth, yet poetic vision to modern witchcraft practice, as well as a greater emphasis on attaining harmony with nature. At the time of her death, on 1 September 1999, she was held in great esteem as the "mother of Wicca" who had contributed to its growth as a religion, to its poetry and to the beauty of its ceremonies and ritual.

*Doreen Valiente, photographed in January 1999.*

Doreen Valiente, who was initiated by Gerald Gardner in 1953 and eventually became his high priestess, has had a great influence on modern witchcraft in the form of rewriting, changing and adapting Gardner's rituals. Valiente discovered Gardner's witchcraft in 1952 when she read an article on "Witchcraft in Britain" published in a magazine.

The article quoted Cecil Williamson, the owner of a witchcraft museum on the Isle of Man. He was talking about witchcraft as the "Old Religion" and telling how the witches in the New Forest had raised a "cone of power" to stop Hitler from invading Britain. Doreen Valiente, who had been interested in magic for many years, wrote to Williamson for information about contacting witches. Williamson passed her letter to Gardner who, after some correspondence, invited her to Dafo's house in Christchurch. There he gave Valiente a copy of his book *High Magic's Aid* to read for information on the witch cult.

Valiente said that her initiation was virtually identical to that described in *High Magic's Aid* except that it included something called "The Charge" (a ritual utterance from an invoked deity) which she recognized as containing passages from Leland's *Aradia* and parts of Aleister Crowley's writings. When she confronted Gardner with the inclusion of this material, he replied that he had had to supplement the fragmentary material from the old coven.

## A REVISED CHARGE

Valiente accepted his challenge to revise the wording of the Charge, removing much of the borrowing from Crowley. It begins with a summons to assemble and adore the Great Mother:

*A witch consecrates the salt with her athame on an altar which includes flowers to link with nature as well as magical symbolism in the pentagram and the flame of the candle.*

*Listen to the words of the Great Mother,
who was of old also called among men,
Artemis, Astarte, Dione, Melusine,
Aphrodite, Cerridwen, Diana,
Arianrhod, Bride, and by
many other names.
At mine Altars the youth of Lacedaemon
in Sparta made due sacrifice.
Whenever ye have need of anything,
once in the month, and better it be
when the moon is full. Then ye shall
assemble in some secret place and
adore the spirit of Me who am
Queen of all Witcheries.
There ye shall assemble, ye who are
fain to learn all sorcery, yet who
have not won its deepest secrets.
To these will I teach things that
are yet unknown ...*

The priestess representing the Goddess identifies herself as the soul of nature:

*I who am the beauty of the green earth;
and the White Moon amongst the Stars;
and the mystery of the Waters; and the
desire of the heart of man, I call unto
thy soul: arise and come unto me.
For I am the Soul of nature who giveth
life to the Universe;
From me all things proceed; and unto
me, all things must return.*

The source of all knowledge lies within:

*And thou who thinkest to seek me,
know that thy seeking and yearning
shall avail thee not unless thou know
the mystery, "That if that which thou
seekest thou findest not within thee,
thou wilt never find it without thee,"
for behold; I have been with thee
from the beginning, and I am that
which is attained at the end of desire.*

Valiente went on to become a formative influence in the development of modern witchcraft, writing a number of books that displayed her own distinct interpretation of the "Old Religion". She recast Gardner's concept of witchcraft as a fertility religion into one that included the mind and the soul, saying that there was a spiritual as well as a material fertility, and that this

*A "Path to Female Empowerment", planted by followers of the Goddess, which illustrates the link between nature and the female.*

*A modern practising witch holding an athame in her right hand and a scourge in her left, in the "Osiris position".*

spiritual fertility was found through finding harmony in nature.

In her later work Doreen Valiente came to distance herself from the position taken by Gerald Gardner, critically describing his version of the craft as rather airy-fairy. She then took instead to working with what she called traditional hereditary witchcraft with Robert Cochrane, who claimed to be a genuine hereditary witch from a long and secret tradition.

*A Wiccan initiation.*

# ALEX SANDERS

At seven years old, Mr Sanders, in an austere and bloody ritual, was initiated into the cult by his grandmother. As a professional, practising witch, and having had first-hand experience with the evils of black witchcraft, which brought him an immense fortune but great personal tragedy, Mr Sanders pledged himself thereafter to the furtherance of witchcraft as a benevolent religion. This is how the cover of Alex Sanders' book of teachings on Alexandrian Wicca introduces its author. A composite of Gardnerian witchcraft and high magic from the hermetic tradition, Alexandrian witchcraft is often considered to be the "high church" of witchcraft, borrowing as it does from the Judaeo-Christian tradition and having elaborate and highly ritualized ceremonies.

*A great showman, Alex Sanders is pictured here with a skull and crossbones.*

Gerald Gardner's original formulation of witchcraft was adopted by his followers, who called themselves "Gardnerians", but a later derivative group, whose members came to be known as "Alexandrians", has come to be especially influential in the development of modern witchcraft. Alex Sanders (1926-1988), the self-proclaimed "King of the Witches", was its founder. He attracted many followers and boasted that he had 1,623 initiates in 100 covens, but little is known about his early involvement with witchcraft and it seems highly likely that he derived most of his material from Gardnerian sources. Sanders, who was born Orrell Alexander Carter in Birkenhead, England, was the eldest of six children, and claimed that he was initiated into witchcraft by his grandmother Mary Bibby, a cunning woman, when he was seven years old. Sanders said that he discovered her standing naked in the middle of a circle drawn on the kitchen floor. Ordering him to enter the circle and to take off his clothes, she made him bend over and cut his scrotum with a knife saying, "You are one of us now".

Sanders spent much of his early life drifting from one job to another, drinking and having sexual liaisons with men and women. After pledging himself to the "left-hand path" or "black magic" and making a fortune, he decided to use his powers for beneficent purposes such as healing. He met Maxine Morris in the 1960s and initiated her into the craft. The couple were handfasted (married) and Maxine became his high priestess.

## PUBLIC WITCHCRAFT

Sanders courted publicity and a film (*Legend of the Witches*), a biography written in 1969 (*King of the Witches*) and his numerous public appearances in the media brought witchcraft into the public eye, much to the dismay of other witches who shunned the association with such showman. He upset many prominent

*Alex Sanders holds a ritual sword during an Alexandrian ritual. Maxine Sanders sits on his right.*

figures, including Patricia Crowther, an initiate of Gardnerian witchcraft. In 1966 Sanders' behaviour prompted Pat Crowther and Ray Bone, another leading spokesperson for witchcraft, to make a public denunciation of Sanders, calling him an impostor because he had not been properly initiated into the Gardnerian witchcraft tradition. This forced Sanders to respond with the story about his initiation by his grandmother. He claimed that hers was the authentic craft, and that Gardner and the Gardnerians were following a later and inferior version.

In fact, Sanders based his version of witchcraft on Gardner's model but incorporated more elements of high magic, being greatly influenced by Eliphas Lévi. Some witches refer to Alexandrian witchcraft as "high church", and Gardnerian witchcraft as "low church". Sanders blurred the boundaries between paganism and Christianity and, according to the historian Ronald Hutton, this marks a distinct difference between the two traditions because Gardner was always concerned to mark a clear separation, preferring to depict himself, like Margaret Murray, as a discoverer of a surviving ancient religious tradition. Alex Sanders and

*An initiation ceremony. Here the prospective candidate is blindfolded and challenged by the high priestess and high priest.*

*Alex Sanders in ritual regalia.*

Maxine Morris, by contrast, portrayed themselves through their life stories as "warriors in a constant battle of good magic against bad". Sanders also placed more emphasis on practical magical techniques such as clairvoyance, astral projection, thought-transference and the use of charms and talismans.

In 1969 a reporter named Stewart Farrar interviewed Sanders for an article in the magazine *Reveille*, and Sanders invited him to attend a witch's initiation. Farrar wrote a two-part feature for the magazine and was sufficiently impressed to become involved himself. He was commissioned to write a book, later published as *What Witches Do*, and he started attending Sanders' training classes. In the Sanders coven he met Janet Owen and they later formed a magical partnership – and their own coven – in 1970. They have published many books on witchcraft.

*A film portrayal of a witchcraft ceremony inspired by Alex Sanders' work.*

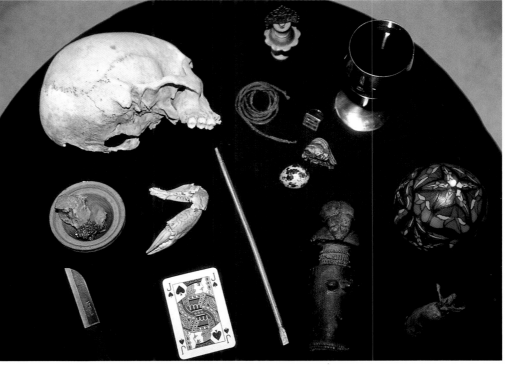

*Witchcraft paraphernalia; skull, wand, chalice, cord, candle, crystals and divination cards.*

# RAYMOND BUCKLAND

It was Raymond Buckland who was largely responsible for taking Gardnerian witchcraft to the United States. An Englishman with Romany blood, Buckland moved to America in 1962 and founded Seax-Wica, a Saxon branch of witchcraft which worships four principle deities: Woden, Thunor, Tiw and Frig or Freya. Buckland had established a relationship with Gerald Gardner when he was living on the Isle of Man and running his witchcraft museum. Impressed with Gardner's museum, Buckland set up a similar one in the United States.

In his introduction to Gardner's book *Witchcraft Today*, Raymond Buckland acknowledged his debt to Gardner, saying that all witches owed Gardner a debt of gratitude for learning his original coven's rituals and adapting them, before breaking from the group and starting his own. Buckland explained that his own life paralleled Gardner's: after being initiated into Gardnerian witchcraft by Gardner's then high priestess Monique Wilson, known as the

Lady Olwen, in Perth, Scotland, he felt it necessary after nearly 12 years to leave this tradition to found his own in the early 1970s. He saw the Saxon tradition of Seax-Wica as a more open branch of Wicca, having no oaths of secrecy.

In Gardnerian witchcraft the high priestess, in partnership with her magical working partner the high priest, is overall leader of her coven. She is seen to be the channel and representative of the Goddess and the coven cannot

*Raymond Buckland in his magic regalia.*

*Raymond Buckland acknowledged his debt to Gardner and adapted many of his rituals.*

function without her or a female representative. By contrast, in Seax-Wica men and women are seen to be equally important and a high priest can act alone. Buckland's version of Wicca has no degrees of advancement and therefore differs from other forms of modern witchcraft, which usually have three initiation degrees (in Alexandrian Wicca the second and third may be taken together). The first is often an introduction to the Goddess, and a time for understanding the unconscious: a man must find aspects of himself in the Goddess, while a woman must absorb qualities that she has projected elsewhere. The second initiation concerns the descent to the underworld, to face fears and find the self. The third initiation concerns the bringing together of all aspects of the person to discover the wisdom within.

## SEAX-WICA

Buckland's system allows for self-initiation by the performance of a rite of self-dedication, after which the initiate may start their own coven. The self-initiate stands with both arms lifted facing an altar and says:

> *Woden and Freya, hear me now!*
> *I am here a simple pagan*
> *holding thee in honor.*
> *Far have I journeyed and long*
> *have I searched,*
> *Seeking that which I desire above all things.*
> *I am of the trees and of the fields.*
> *I am of the woods and of the springs;*
> *The streams and the hills.*
> *I am of thee; and thee of me ...*

However, it is preferred that the initiate is introduced and trained in the customary manner, and there are three categories of relative involvement in Seax-Wica. The first is the Theows: those who do not belong to the Saxon craft, but attend the rituals by invitation. This introduction may lead to a request for further involvement and training leading to initiation, when the neophyte is termed a Ceorl. After a period of time – anything from a month to a year depending on the person's spiritual

*A Wiccan Samhain (Hallowe'en) ceremony with the high priestess crowning the high priest.*

development – the neophyte is initiated and becomes a Gesith, after which there is no further degree of advancement. Buckland claims that this counters any tendency for one person to become too powerful, and helps to stop any egoism developing. Recognizing that it was not

possible for everyone to go through the course of training, Buckland tried to make the craft more accessible to earnest seekers. He started many covens and established the Seax-Wica Seminary correspondence school in Virginia in the early 1970s, later moving to San Diego. He has written many books about witchcraft but has subsequently turned his attention to writing about Gypsies. He notes that the Romany word for "witch" is "shuvihani" (the masculine form is "shuvihano") meaning "wise one", the implication being that the witch is knowledgable in all aspects of the occult. A shuvihani has experience of magical beliefs and practices; she is not considered evil in any way. Many shuvihanis undertake a vision quest similar to that of Native Americans to gain previously unknown knowledge.

Thus Buckland has, as a "poshrat", or half-blood Romany, sought to understand and practise both witchcraft and gypsy magic. Like Alex Sanders he adapted Gardnerian witchcraft to his own ideas and experience. In this sense Wicca has proved to be a flexible set of techniques open to much interpretation.

*Wiccan high priest and priestess of the Gardnerian tradition, the foundation for Buckland's own interpretation of witchcraft.*

# HEREDITARY WITCHCRAFT

While most witches now accept that their religion is a modern recreation of paganism that links back to the past spiritually rather than historically, others reject this and assert that their practices have been handed down through family tradition. Many of the beliefs and practices of hereditary witches can be traced back to the work of Charles Godfrey Leland, and his research on the supposedly secret religion of witches who worshipped the goddess Diana and the god Lucifer.

It is now fairly well estblished that modern witchcraft was formulated in the early 1950s. A significant minority, however, claim that they do belong to an unbroken inherited tradition that comes to them through their own family rather than any social inheritance. Scholarship on this subject has so far failed to provide any proof to support these claims. Most hereditary witches draw on the work of Margaret Murray and her view that the Old Religion was a fragmented form of pagan religion, which had managed to survive centuries of Christian persecution. Others claim that their traditions stem directly from the Italian witchcraft explored in the writings of Charles Godfrey Leland, especially his book *Aradia: Gospel of the Witches*, published in 1899.

### THE COCHRANE COVEN

Robert Cochrane claimed that he was a hereditary witch who was initiated at the age of five, his practice passing through his family. A former blacksmith, he named his coven the Clan of the Tubal Cain after a smith in Hebrew legend. Doreen Valiente, who was initiated into Gardnerian Wicca in 1953, co-wrote a book called *Witchcraft: A Tradition Renewed* (1990) with another initiate from Cochrane's coven, Evan John Jones, to put forward basic ways of working according to this tradition.

An ideal coven structure consisted of 13 members: six men and six women, with the Lady – who directed proceedings, dedicated the circle, led celebrants in, dedicated the cakes and wine, and closed the ritual – as the thirteenth.

Each of the correspondences had an officer associated with it: the north was attended by the "Dark One", the Hag; the south by the Mother aspect of the Goddess; the east by a young man who symbolized light; the west by a male guardian of the gates of the underworld. The rest of the coven was made up of initiates and apprentices, who served an apprenticeship of a year and a day. A "Man in Black" maintained contact between covens; and a "Summoner", while keeping contact with the Man in Black, acted as a record-keeper and also organized such things as transport to ritual sites. Cochrane's coven followed a Gardnerian pattern of rites – celebrating

*Lucifer, or the Devil, is another representation of the horned god or Pan, the goat-footed god of nature, life and vitality.*

*Tradition is an important part of modern magic and much folklore and many beliefs are passed on through museums, such as this witchcraft museum in Cornwall.*

the Great Sabbats of Candlemas, May Eve, Lammas, and Hallowe'en, and also the Lesser Sabbats of the equinoxes and solstices – but there were also important differences. They assigned air to the north (earth in Gardnerian Wicca), earth to the south (fire in the Gardnerian tradition) and fire to the east (air in Gardnerian Wicca), while the west was associated with water as in the Gardnerian tradition. Ronald Hutton noted that there was more emphasis upon the God as Lord of Death than in Gardner's tradition, and that the Man in Black or "Magister" functioned as high priest in the role of divine sacrificial king; in this he was supported by the Maid or Lady. The Magister also conducted a rite before the ceremonial consumption of cakes and wine, dipping his knife into a cup of wine in which the moon was reflected by the use of a mirror. Doreen Valiente noted that Cochrane's rituals were more spontaneous and shamanistic, more earthy than those of Gardner, and that this was partly because the coven did not use a Book of Shadows in which to record rituals, leading to more creativity.

*A hereditary coven will often work its rituals and celebrations outside.*

# Charles Leland

Raven Grimassi used the works of Charles Godfrey Leland, particularly *Aradia* (the Italianized name of Herodias, who was portrayed as a villain in the New Testament for her part in the death of John the Baptist) to trace the alleged origins of his craft. Leland wrote that the Italian witch came from a family in which her calling or art had been practised for many generations. In 1886 he had met a woman called Maddelena who claimed to be a witch. She had apparently inherited a collection of family charms and invocations that could heal, break curses and invoke certain spirits. Leland used these and employed her as a research assistant to find out more about the secret religion of the witches. In particular he sought to find the gospel of its body of beliefs, and eventually Maddelena managed to provide him with such a manuscript obtained from oral sources. What Leland considered to be an ancient pagan religion was thus recorded.

*A portrait of Charles Godfrey Leland.*

*The frontispiece of Leland's seminal and highly influential work,* Aradia.

Ronald Hutton concluded that Cochrane used a Wiccan framework to develop his own ideas and practices, and called it hereditary witchcraft.

Cochrane's hereditary legacy lives on in a coven named the Regency, which was formed on Hallowe'en in 1966 by two former members of Cochrane's coven. They combined his ideas with those of Ruth Wynn Owen, who also claimed to be a hereditary witch coming from a family with psychic skills whose rituals were similar to Wicca in their veneration of a God and Goddess. The hereditary craft spread to America through the work of Joseph Wilson, who developed the "1734 tradition", a special numerological value based on Robert Graves' *The White Goddess* (1948).

## RAVEN GRIMASSI

Also claiming to be a hereditary witch in the "Strega Tradition" of old Italy, Raven Grimassi was taught by his mother about the Old Religion. He says that the old faith is based on the belief that spirits inhabit both physical objects and all of nature, and that he learnt that it was possible to call up the fairy folk. This was done by pouring milk, honey and wine into a bowl, putting it under a myrtle bush and then swinging a reed tied to a string in a clockwise circle while whistling. A rustling of the leaves signified that the fairies had come.

## DIANA

The old faith focused on deities personified as the great Goddess, represented by Diana, and the horned god, represented by Lucifer. The myth of Diana tells that she was the first to be created and in her were all things. She divided herself into darkness and light: her brother and son Dianus was her other half and was the light, while she was the dark. When Diana saw the beauty of the light she yearned for it and swallowed it up in delight. This desire was the dawn. However, Dianus fled from her and would not yield to her wishes. Diana lamented to the Fathers of the Beginning, to the Mothers and the Spirits, and they told her that to rise she must fall and that therefore she had to become

*The goddess Diana is closely associated with the moon in hereditary witchcraft. She is seen here in part of a series of reliefs depicting the planetary symbols and signs of the zodiac.*

*Diana is always depicted as a beautiful goddess with an essentially feminine aspect.*

54

mortal. So Diana descended to earth with Dianus, where she taught magic and sorcery; thus witches and magicians came to be. Her brother Dianus had a cat, which slept on his bed. One day Diana took the form of a cat like her brother's; she lay with her brother and in the darkness assumed her own form. This is how Diana became the mother of Aradia. Dianus was angry, but Diana sang a spell to keep him silent. She hummed a song like the buzzing of bees and the spinning of a wheel. Like a spinning wheel spinning life, she spun the lives of men. All things are said to be spun from the wheel of Diana, while Dianus turned the wheel.

Grimassi says that the Gardnerian tradition took on elements of Italian witchcraft from the works of Charles Leland: part of the Charge of the Goddess contains elements of Leland's material, and other borrowings are full-moon gatherings, worship of a goddess, ritual celebrations involving cakes and wine and worshipping naked.

*According to some, Wiccan ritual celebrations may have been inspired by traditions that were handed down by hereditary witchcraft.*

*Some hereditary witches say that Gardnerian witches borrowed elements – such as worshipping naked – from their tradition.*

# FEMINIST WITCHCRAFT

Feminist witchcraft is a later variant of modern witchcraft. It is now primarily associated with the work of Starhawk, an influential figure in feminist witchcraft, and has a strong political dimension. Feminist witches often work with what they term ecstasy, rather than the feminine/masculine polarity, which is central to Gardnerian Wicca. Magical work for social change – to end patriarchal oppression – is also a predominant part of their rituals.

*Jules Michelet, the French historian who studied the records of the witch hunters.*

In the 1970s the women's liberation movement produced a general critique of world religions, which, it was said, denied women's experience. Two differing branches of feminist spirituality emerged: those keen to reform orthodox religions and those who looked to pre-Christian goddesses such as those celebrated in modern witchcraft. Ideas of the witch as a freedom fighter against patriarchy were used by American radical feminists. According to Rachel Hasted, writing in the magazine *Trouble and Strife* (1985), the original WITCH (Women Inspired To Commit Herstory) group accepted ready-made "facts" about the witch-craze in Europe and claimed that nine million witches had been burned as revolutionary fighters against patriarchy and class oppression. They drew on the work of Jules Michelet, Joslyn Gage and Margaret Murray. Each of these writers had contributed to the idea that there was an underground movement of women's spirituality, originating from matriarchal times, which had been suppressed.

The French historian Jules Michelet's *La Sorcière* (1862) had interpreted witch hunters' records as a massive peasant rebellion and rejection of Christianity in which pagan priestesses led a doomed peasants' revolt against the oppression of a Christian ruling class. Matilda Joslyn Gage, a radical leader of the US suffrage movement, had argued in *Woman, Church and State* (1893) that witchcraft and the occult were a form of knowledge that was based on the worship of a female deity which had been outlawed by a jealous patriarchy. Margaret Murray's *The Witch-Cult in Western Europe* (1921) had claimed that European witchcraft was an ancient pre-Christian fertility religion, which had survived among the peasantry.

Feminist witchcraft's mythical origins lie in a golden woman-centred age before patriarchal religions came to dominate both women and nature. Judaeo-Christian traditions were seen to have deepened the split, finally establishing a duality between spirit and matter. Women became identified with matter, nature, the body, sexuality, evil and the Devil, and had to be controlled, while the male God was uncontaminated by birth, menstruation and decay and was removed to the realm of the spirit. Feminist witchcraft, in common with Wicca, has a holistic vision of the world: the Goddess is seen to link people with nature; she is seen to be within every human being and her worship involves celebrating life: she is associated with renewal and the regeneration of life.

The origins of Goddess-worship are traced to ancient, peaceful, egalitarian cultures where the change of seasons and lunar and solar cycles were experienced as mystic bonds linking humanity with nature. Much of this feminist reinterpretation of witchcraft is based on the work of the archaeologist Marija Gimbutas, who attributed a single religious system of Goddess-worship to both palaeolithic hunter-gatherers and neolithic farmers and horticulturalists. Gimbutas claimed that when food-gathering gave way to food-producing, leading to a settled way of life, there was no corresponding change in the religious symbolism – the Goddess ruled throughout. According to Gimbutas, this peaceable old European culture was overrun by violent patriarchal invasions between 4300 and 2800BC. The anthropologist Ruby Rohrlich disagrees with this view and

*The old stereotype of the witch shown in this illustration has recently been recast by feminists.*

points to the earliest civilizations in Sumer, Egypt, India and China, and also the societies of the Incas and the Aztecs, claiming that they gradually transformed themselves from peaceable, women-centred enclaves into warring, stratified cultures. She argues that the changes were made from within rather than by patriarchal invaders from without. Nevertheless, the idea that there was a peaceful, Goddess-focused, pre-patriarchal society is very common among feminist witches.

## ZSUZSANNA BUDAPEST (1940–)

In 1971, "women's mysteries" were created in Malibu, USA. According to Zsuzsanna Budapest, a group of women sat around a weatherbeaten old café table eating eggs and potatoes, drinking coffee, talking and fantasizing and laughing, and knowing that they were doing something revolutionary that was going to influence the world. Budapest, who claims that she comes from a long line of witches, and that she is the "last branch of an 800-year-old family tree", says that her mother Masika was the result of an immaculate conception, and was taught all the arts of witchcraft by a very well-known witch from Transylvania.

# Spiritual Suffrage

The Susan B. Anthony Coven No.1 was started by Zsuzsanna Budapest on the winter solstice in 1971 in Hollywood. It was named after the suffragist Susan B. Anthony, a leading campaigner for women's suffrage and president of the National American Woman's Suffrage Association. When Anthony was asked what she would do in the afterlife, she reputedly answered "When I die, I shall go neither to heaven nor hell, but stay right here and finish the women's revolution", a comment that inspired Budapest to acknowledge Anthony as an ancestress, whose work should be honoured and continued.

*The American feminist Susan B. Anthony.*

Budapest was part of a Malibu core group of eight women who created what has been termed the "Dianic tradition" of feminist witchcraft by celebrating rituals together and contributing their experiences to *The Holy Book of Women's Mysteries* (1989). Dianic tradition witches are usually either celibate or lesbian.

This form of witchcraft is based on Wicca and shares its structure: the coven is composed of up to 13; sabbaths are held on the same festivals; the ritual structure is based on a circle and four quarters. Other similarities are the emphasis on feasting and sexuality; witches are supposed to enter the circle "in perfect love and perfect trust"; the naked body is seen to represent truth; and the abiding moral maxim is "Do as thou wilt and harm none". The main differences focus on the central role of politics and an emphasis on democratic working (whereas Gardner's system was based on a hierarchical, initiatory system of three degrees); and the primacy of the Goddess, sometimes to the total exclusion of the God.

Feminist politics have been central to the practice from the start and Budapest speaks of the difficulties of combining religion with politics in the early days. For Budapest, spirituality concerns the struggle to liberate the religious woman inside by the creation of a faith system that will serve women. She has written that in the true beginning, before the Judaeo-Christian Genesis, "the Goddess was revealed to her people as the Soul of the Wild. Called Holy Mother, she was known to be a Virgin who lived in wild places and acted through mysterious powers. Known also as Artemis, She was worshipped in the moonlight, and young nymphs and maidens were called to serve in Her rituals. The Holy Mother, Virgin, Artemis was also called by the name Dia Anna, 'Nurturer Who Does Not Bear Young'."

*Women and the earth are seen as especially sacred in feminist and Goddess spirituality. This is a ritual at the Goddess Festival in Glastonbury, England, honouring the powers of nature.*

*Starhawk leading a spiral dance in America: she is the central figure holding a drum. The spiral dance gathers everyone and engenders a feeling of collectivity and connectedness.*

## STARHAWK (1951–)

Starhawk (Miriam Simos), the woman who has had the most formative effect on feminist witchcraft, attended her first ritual with the Susan B. Anthony Coven, according to Budapest. Starhawk's background is Jewish and she still sees herself as Jewish but she sought an alternative spirituality because "in Judaism there were no images of powerful women". She also had powerful spiritual experiences, which did not fit Judaism because they "seemed to take place in nature or in the context of sexuality", and in traditional Jewish circles at this time these were not discussed.

## THE FAERY TRADITION

In 1975 Starhawk began to study with Victor Anderson and was initiated into the Faery (Feri) tradition as taught by him. Victor Anderson and Gwydion Pendderwen founded the Faery tradition of witchcraft, and it is likely that Anderson was influenced by Margaret Murray's work on fairies. Anderson was allegedly initiated into the craft by witches who called themselves faeries, and he worked in covens with people from southern America and practised a "devotional science", harmonizing with nature, performing magic and engaging in ecstatic dancing. Anderson was also

initiated into the Harpy coven in Oregon in 1932. This was eclectic, mixing Huna from Hawaii with varieties of folk magic more common in the rest of the United States. There was an emphasis on practical magic and little concern with worship, theology, ethics or ritual.

According to the Faery tradition, there is a Mother-Father God called the "Drychton" (after the Anglo-Saxon word for "lord" or "ruler") who is the male-female power, being both the God and the Goddess. In the beginning, according to the mythology, the light from the stars bounced off the curved mirror of space in the directions of left and right and produced the other deities: the gods on one side and the goddesses on the other. Above all, the Faery tradition is an ecstatic one – rather than one that is based on fertility, as in Gardner's original formulation of Wicca – and the aim is to become one with the gods. The sexes are seen to be equal and there is no high priestess in overall charge. Later, Alexandrian witchcraft material was incorporated into the tradition.

In her first work, *The Spiral Dance: A rebirth of the ancient religion of the Great Goddess* (1979), Starhawk located the origins of Goddess-religion in peaceful neolithic Europe, which suffered attack from patriarchal Indo-European warrior tribes. Starhawk's view of the history of the "Goddess peoples", which is heavily influenced by the now discredited theories of Margaret Murray, is based on their escape from persecution from waves of invasion by warrior gods, who drove the Goddess peoples out of the

*Another performance of the sacred spiral dance, this time in Glastonbury, England. The dance begins with all the participants holding hands and beginning a winding snake-like movement around the room, during which a complex pattern allows everyone to have contact with each other at some point.*

fertile lowlands into the hills and high mountains, where they became known as the sidhe, pixies, fair folk or faeries.

Murray had claimed, in *The Witch-Cult in Western Europe* (1921), that witch beliefs were associated with an early European dwarf race, which at one time inhabited Europe and survived in stories of fairies and elves, and that every seven years they made a human sacrifice to their god. According to Murray, fairies gradually became identified with witches. Both fairies and witches were said to cast and break spells, heal, divine for lost objects and the future, "traffick" with the Devil, change shape, fly, levitate and steal unbaptized children.

Starhawk builds up a picture of the faeries based on the ideas of Victor Anderson and Margaret Murray. According to her version, the faeries preserved the pre-Christian, pre-patriarchal Old Religion. They bred cattle in the stony hills and lived in turf-covered round huts. Clan mothers, called Queens of Elphame, led covens, together with a priest, the sacred king, who embodied the dying God who died a mock death at the end of his term of office. They celebrated the eight festivals of the wheel of the year with "wild processions on horseback, singing, chanting, and the lighting of ritual fires". Starhawk writes that the sacred king, or high priest, held office for nine years, after which he underwent a ritual death, abdicated and joined the council of elders.

## POLITICS

There is a political thread running through all of Starhawk's writing. She contrasts a peaceful vision of society in which all are honoured and live in empathy with the natural world, with a culture based on the dominance of some people over others and the destruction of the environment. In *Dreaming the Dark* (1982) she says that the "burning times", when women were persecuted as witches in Europe, were linked to a stealing of common land, natural resources and knowledge by a culture based on what she calls a "consciousness of estrangement". She contrasts this with the "consciousness of immanence",

*The Goddess is worshipped in many guises. Here a "black Madonna" is venerated at the Goddess festival in Glastonbury.*

which she claims is found in women, sexuality and magic. In her next book, *Truth or Dare* (1990), she focused on ancient Sumerian Mesopotamia, and wrote about a spiritual battle of power between the priestesses of the temple and the king. Initially, she says, these roles were elected and based on an equal relationship, ritually maintained, but eventually the king usurped power: refusing to relinquish his kingship to an elected successor, he passed it on to his sons instead. This changed the relationship with the priestesses of the temple, and relations with women in general, by establishing an oppressive patriarchy with its consciousness of estrangement. In her novels *The Fifth Sacred Thing* (1993), which is set in the

year 2040, and *Walking to Mercury* (1997), which is a fictionalized autobiography, Starhawk finally developed the "fantasy of a living future", which is briefly outlined at the end of *Truth or Dare*. Starhawk's works offer a vision of the future by using the imagination, which is the basis of magic, to envision a different reality.

Moving away from Dianic witchcraft, Starhawk includes men in her version of witchcraft. However, men have to learn how to be non-oppressive and how to discover, or rediscover, the parts of themselves that have been repressed by patriarchy. Starhawk's vision of witchcraft combines political activism and therapeutic techniques within a spiritual system loosely based on Wicca.

# WESTERN MAGIC TODAY

Western magical practices, including modern witchcraft, offer a kaleidoscope of paths or techniques for attaining alternative forms of consciousness. All of these attempt to go beyond ordinary, everyday awareness to achieve a heightened state which some, such as high magicians who practise "Western mysteries", describe as contact with a deity or angels. Others, such as chaos magicians, strive to achieve an altered state of consciousness by deconditioning the self to obtain inner knowledge. Many, but not all, of those who have an interest in Western magic see the world in a spiritual way, and so the link that magic has had with religion in the past is still in evidence.

# TODAY'S MAGICIANS

By using a variety of different techniques, magicians learn to see themselves as part of a magical whole – a wider pattern underlying all of life, including the seen and the unseen. There are many different paths – from the various forms of modern witchcraft, where people of either sex work alone or with others, to New Age, which has a very wide variety of different expressions and beliefs. What these different branches of Western magic share is that most followers and practitioners seek communication with what is often termed the "otherworld", a realm of spirit beings, defined or personalized in many ways. A trained magician can move in and out of contact with the otherworld with facility, in much the same way as shamans have done in times past, and still do today.

*Modern Western magic often forms an alternative religious or spiritual practice today, and much of the symbolism remains the same.*

Who are the people who practise magic today in Western cultures? To call them magicians is likely to conjure up an image of Tolkien's Gandalf striding into the unknown, staff in hand, long robes and hair flowing in the wind. This romantic image has currency among those who practise magic, helping to add glamour and bring mystery into many magical traditions. Alternatively, magicians may be seen as Satanists, evildoers, part of a malevolent cosmic force working against God and the forces of good. Neither of these images are how most modern magicians see themselves, and most would strongly assert that they use magical powers for healing and positive purposes rather than for negative or destructive ends. There are many magical practices and paths to choose from today. A glance at the noticeboard in a local occult or New Age bookstore will reveal advertisements for courses, groups, healing, astrological consultation and much more; as will any of a number of specialist magazines. It is possible to join a witchcraft coven, train as a high or ceremonial magician in an occult school, become a druid, engage in a whole variety of New Age activities, practise Western forms of shamanism, perform magical rituals within the Northern or Nordic tradition, or become a chaos magician. These magical groups and traditions offer a kaleidoscope of ways of engaging in magic.

A magical world-view is a different way of seeing the world; it is holistic – often viewed as an interconnected web of forces and energies, which may be communicated and worked with, or controlled and directed. Each magical tradition will have a slightly different

*White-robed druids celebrating Spring Equinox at Tower Hill, London, by sowing seed and making blessings for new life.*

emphasis and way of working. For example, witches may prefer to work outside in nature, while high magicians may work in a specially consecrated temple dedicated to Egyptian deities, and a modern Western shamanic practitioner may go on spirit journeys conducted within a drumming circle. Many modern magical practices have adopted the eight seasonal festivals of the year developed by Gerald Gardner and his druid friend Ross Nichols. These festivals are seen to be the points where the magician links in with the wider forces of the cosmos. This is based on the understanding that the human being, as magician, witch, druid or shaman, is part of a wider pattern of life. This pattern of life includes the unseen as well as the seen.

Some magical practices offer training and a series of graduated initiations as part of a process for opening up awareness of magical forces and energies. By using various different techniques, such as meditation, guided path-workings or visionary journeys, the initiate is encouraged to value and focus on realities that are not always apparent in the everyday, ordinary world. This may mean learning to experience and

feel using intuition as well as using the critical faculties of the mind; it also involves learning to see significant connections between what would previously have been seen as separate events. It concerns coming to value the

*Not all magical practices are viewed as spiritual traditions. This Baphomet statue is celebrated by chaos magicians who see magic primarily as a technique for changing consciousness.*

*Modern witchcraft can be practised in many different ways. People work alone or together and are free to formulate their own rituals.*

connections of the whole as part of a spiritual journey that leads into another reality. This reality is often called the "otherworld" and it may be described in terms of spirits, deities and a whole range of other beings that are believed to inhabit this other dimension. Communication with the otherworld is possible through the active imagination, when the mind is in a state of light trance. The otherworld is said to co-exist with the ordinary world, and a trained magician can move in and out of these different forms of awareness with ease.

*An important part of many magical practices is being able to see the seen and the unseen. Here, a crystal ball is being used to access the deeper parts of consciousness to gain what is seen to be spiritual truth.*

# WESTERN MYSTERIES

Modern magic's central ethos is working with the idea of spiritual evolution – the bringing down of higher angelic or elemental forces into the magician. This bringing down is a process that is thought to enable the soul to evolve; an idea which has been at the centre of much religious thought. Practitioners of Western Mysteries often work with esoteric versions of Christianity to seek unity with God. They may also use Egyptian myths, such as that of Isis and Osiris, to access what they see as deep levels of inner knowledge and wisdom in the name of spiritual and divine truth, or the legends and myths of other cultures, such as the British Arthurian legends.

*Angels play an important role in Western magical traditions.*

High or ceremonial magic, or "Western Mysteries", is a form of European magic distinguished by modern magicians from eastern magical systems. For those magicians who practise the Western Mysteries, all life forms – animals, plants, rocks – are evolving, but human beings are often seen as the supreme carriers of divinity, and they consequently have a responsibility to other life forms.

Magical rituals are frequently based on mythological themes and cycles concerning life and death, such as those of Isis and Osiris, and the descent into the underworld as undergone by Persephone. Each myth is seen to reveal a deeper inner truth. Western Mysteries are a magical form of Neoplatonism whereby the individual soul of the magician seeks reunion with the divine One. This frequently encompasses versions of esoteric Christianity which seek unity with divinity after the Fall, and concerns the mastery of the lower self and baser nature in the spiritual pursuit of the Ultimate Being. This is seen in terms of a union of the magician's soul with the One. It is said that the primordial teachings came from Egypt and were derived from the lost island of Atlantis.

The Western Mysteries are usually taught in occult schools and have initiation schemes whereby the apprentice may progress to a number of different levels or degrees, each of which

*Each angel is seen as a being of pure consciousness in profound union with God.*

has an appropriate outward insignia – for example, a distinctively coloured robe or girdle. Western Mystery magical work is usually focused on working with cabbalistic path workings or meditation on certain spheres of the tree of life. Group rituals are conducted in a lodge or a temple dedicated to a deity.

## ANGELS

Most Western Mystery schools work with the idea of spiritual evolution and the bringing down of higher angelic forces into the magician to aid the soul's progress. This developed from the Hermetic tradition, which attempted to rise above the deceptions of sense by attunement to the divine mind through the contemplation of the universe. The practice is concerned with raising a fallen human nature in a wider movement of spiritual evolution. According to the high magician David Goddard, from the One, which is beyond understanding or comprehension, comes an overflowing of eternal love that expresses itself in a multitude of beings. The One is a creator and through this overflowing of love comes creation. The One becomes many – the seven great spirits of the Elohim, seven princes, archangels or "lords of flame": the Elohim form a prism through which the One is refracted and through which the One acts. Each angel is a being of pure consciousness and is in profound union with the One, beyond time or space, channelling the divine light without distortion. An angel is a focus of power, wisdom, beauty and love, and they have a teaching function. For David Goddard, Michael helps in matters of achievement and ambition; Gabriel is concerned with psychic development; Samael is invoked for courage or perseverence; Raphael is a specialist in healing and communication; Sachiel helps in financial matters; Asariel rules in mediumship and trancework; Haniel is associated with the devas of nature; Cassiel supervises the energies of the planet; and Uriel transmits the Magical Force. Thus angels can be invoked in times of trouble or consternation to give practical and spiritual insight.

*Some modern magicians use Egyptian myths as part of their magical practices.*

*Angels are called on to help in a whole range of human concerns and dilemmas.*

## THE ARTHURIAN LEGEND

The mythology of King Arthur and his Knights of the Round Table is important to magicians following the Western Mysteries because, like most other mythologies, they provide a moral and spiritual model on which to base magical practice.

Arthur is a Celtic hero, the son of King Uther Pendragon and the Lady Igraine, and his birth was made possible by the magical workings of Merlin the magician. The earliest written historical record of Arthur is in the *Historia Brittonum* (compiled in the early ninth century) which says that "the warrior Arthur" fought with the kings of the Britons against the Saxons, whom he conquered in 12 battles conducted in the sixth century. Arthur's entry into legend was effected by Geoffrey of Monmouth, who mixed these historical fragments with local traditions and Celtic myth. Consequently, Arthur and Merlin are hybrids, blending historical people with mythological characters.

## THE ROMANCE OF ARTHUR

According to legend, Arthur was a fifth-century Christianized British warrior who made a stand against the barbarian Anglo-Saxon invaders from Denmark and Germany when Roman rule collapsed in 400AD. Writing in the twelfth century, Geoffrey of Monmouth portrayed Arthur's reign as the climax of the history of the kings of Britain. Drawing on Welsh monastic writing, Breton folklore, poems and legends, he created the realm of Arthur as a piece of literary fiction. Arthur came to preside over a court with complex codes of etiquette and expression: jousts and combats were conducted under strict

*As King Arthur dies, the lady of the lake receives his sword, Excalibur, from Sir Bedivere.*

moral and ethical rules of behaviour. The language of courtly love was based on the theme of unattainable passion – the beloved was seen to embody the image of the divine and was married to another. Underpinning the whole was a deeper dimension of the spiritual quest: the court was the point of departure for adventures into the otherworld.

The Round Table was set up by Merlin and had places for 150 knights, who were all equal in rank and loyal to King Arthur, who was first among equals. The knights embarked on quests, venturing deep into primeval forests, and these were metaphors for the soul's journey through uncharted

*The central magical figure of the Arthurian legends is Merlin. Here, he comes under the enchantment of the Lady Nimue, the female magic figure who inherited his wisdom and who acts as a benign counterbalance to Arthur's sister, the malevolent sorceress, Morgan le Fey.*

worlds. The quest is an archetypal image of a spiritual search for the soul: Jason's quest for the golden fleece and Dante's wanderings in the dark forest to find an earthly paradise are but two examples. The goal of the quest could be a person, such as a maiden in distress, or a divine object such as the Holy Grail.

## THE QUEST FOR THE GRAIL

The Grail is a complex symbol with many meanings. Allegedly the cup from the Last Supper used to collect the blood of Christ, it was said to have been brought from Palestine to Britain via Spain and North Africa by Joseph of Arimathea. It is associated with Glastonbury in Somerset, sometimes called the sacred Isle of Avalon, where Joseph of Arimathea founded the first Christian community. The Grail is seen to be a sacred vessel that contains the potentiality of all wisdom, intuition and knowledge; it is also thought to be the source of creativity and inspiration; it is a magical chalice of transformation, a cauldron of rebirth. It is thought to be able to effect a form of spiritual alchemy, bringing about a higher form of consciousness; it is held that it can bring healing; it is also symbolic of the female power of the womb, and of the Goddess. The myth of King Arthur offers magicians a range of heroic patterns or archetypes with which to identify in a personal quest for a higher form of consciousness whereby the ordinary, everyday consciousness is dissolved, purification ensues, and the individual soul is reunited with the One.

## AN ETHICAL MODEL

The Arthurian legend and the figures within it are important components of the Western Mysteries for many magicians. This is because the Western Mysteries are a form of Neoplatonism – a philosophical view of the world that gives a view of the universe and explains the human position within it. Above all, it outlines how human beings can achieve salvation by restoring their original divine nature in union with God. Arthurian mythology offers a moral and ethical model for this purpose.

*The Grail was allegedly the cup used by Jesus and his disciples at the Last Supper, and then later to collect the blood of Christ during his crucifixion. Once thought of as a mark of spiritual purity, the Grail today represents the potentiality of all wisdom, intuition and creativity for many magicians.*

*Symbolic of magical transformation, the Grail represents a form of spiritual alchemy to bring about a higher form of consciousness. This twelfth-century depiction shows the cup standing at the centre of the round table, another very potent symbol within the Arthurian legend.*

# DRUIDRY

The druids are thought to have been Celtic spiritual leaders, but exactly who they were and what they did remains unknown. What information is available comes from Roman sources, but pagan Celtic beliefs were intensely localized and few generalizations can be made. It is clear that the druids have been imagined in various ways in different periods, from the Renaissance to the Romantic movement, and more recently in the 1970s as part of the general expansion of spiritualities in Western cultures. Once only associated with men in white robes, celebrating the solstice at Stonehenge, today druidry is interpreted more widely as a spirituality in touch with nature.

*Stonehenge is particularly associated with the druids, as this nineteenth-century aquatint shows.*

The esoteric origins of modern druidism are located in the Western Mystery mythological tradition. Philip Carr-Gomm, the current chief of the Order of Bards, Ovates and Druids, says that the magicians of Atlantis discovered the secrets of nature and worked in tune with her powers. However, some used their powers for selfish ends and there developed a struggle between good, or white, magic and bad, or black, magic. The battle lines were drawn between those who saw in nature the great divine Mother of men who used her gifts for human welfare, and those who saw nature as a Satanic temptress with cruel power. As catastrophe struck Atlantis, the dark lords were engulfed while the white sages, having greater gifts of foreknowledge, journeyed both east and west. In the west they landed on the shore of America, and in the east, on the shores of Ireland and the western coasts of Britain, and so druidry spread.

*Human sacrifices were said to have been put in wicker-work images and burned by the Celts, supposedly to promote the fertility of the land.*

## DRUID FESTIVALS

Today, modern druids celebrate the same eight festivals as witches. In druidism these are called: Samhuinn (31 October–2 November), Winter Solstice or Alban Arthuan (Light of Arthur), Imbolc or Oimelc (2 February), Spring Equinox or Beltane (1 May), Summer Solstice or Alban Heruin (21 or 22 June), Lughnasadh (1 August) and Autumnal Equinox or Alban Elued (21 September). Of these festivals, Samhuinn is the time when "the veil between this world and the World of the Ancestors is drawn aside" and druids prepare to make contact with the spirits of the departed as living spirits of loved ones who hold the "root wisdom of the tribe" as a source of guidance. There is much variety in druid rituals and they differ from group to group. Sometimes members adapt or completely rewrite rituals for their own use. According to Philip Shallcrass, the British Druid Order rituals are based on the story of Lleu Llaw Gyffes in the *Mabinogion*, a collection of supposedly Welsh Celtic myths. According to Ronald Hutton, however, they were popular international tales with their origins in Egypt, India or China, which had spread across Asia and Europe and were mixed with Irish and British myths. They were put in their final form by a courtly entertainer by the late eleventh century, when they were probably not more than a century or two old.

## DRUID BELIEF SYSTEMS

Shallcrass points out that there is no central druid theology but that two generalizations about druid beliefs can be made: the first is that there is a belief in a power or energy resident in the earth or in nature, which is often represented as a mother, but it is left to individuals to decide how they wish to look upon this entity; the second is that there is some kind of unified force underlying the manifest world, but again that force is defined by each individual.

Emma Restall-Orr, joint chief with Philip Shallcrass of the British Druid Order, says that druidism includes a whole spectrum of beliefs but that a love of the earth is what holds druids together. Restall-Orr describes druidism as an animistic faith, not a "call of the gods". Communing with nature means learning to grow, to trust and to hear the response of the earth. Nature as deity is drawn down into the ritual circle and this is experienced as joy and love. The internalization of love, joy and inspiration is called "Awen" in modern druidism, and it is the role of bards – as poets and musicians – to encourage the flow of Awen. Ovates, or vates, have a different function: they listen to the voices of the otherworld using various forms of divination such as tree lore and

*Modern druids celebrate dawn within the circle at Stonehenge at the Summer Solstice or Alban Heruin. A vigil is held through the night and as dawn breaks a ceremony marks the sun's rising. A further ritual is held at noon.*

*Emma Restall-Orr, joint chief of the British Druid Order.*

runes. Ovates are facilitators, healers, "changers of situations", and their role is to interpret signs and ask questions. Tree lore is associated with a symbolic language called Ogham (pronounced o'um), which links a tree with a letter of the alphabet, and runes are a series of symbols often inscribed on wood or stone. They are associated with the Norse god Odin, who hung upside down on the cosmic tree Yggdrasil, and through his suffering came to understand the cosmic meaning of the universe, which he then revealed to humans through the runes. Modern druidism is a quest for a spirituality that connects the individual with the natural world through artistic expression and inspiration.

## THE DRUIDS' HISTORY

Modern druidism developed from the late eighteenth-century Romantic movement, but this was not the first time that the druids had been "discovered". Stuart Piggott shows that from the Renaissance onwards those steeped in the philosophy and scholarship of the Greek and Roman thinkers had sought to rediscover the beliefs and practices of the druids. In the eighteenth century, when "fashion shifted from classical to

romantic, the druids were quietly waiting to take on a new life in the contemporary modes of Western thought and emotion". The druid story has an evidential basis in archaeology and what can be deduced of ancient Celtic religion from texts and iconography. In searching for the origins of the druids, Piggott has outlined three types of source material. The first is archaeological evidence from graves, ceremonial sites or representations in Celtic or Romano-Celtic art; the second is the writings of Greeks and Romans on the Celts; and the third is the development of ideas about the druids that originated in the antiquarian speculations of the seventeenth and eighteenth centuries, and were used by scholars as well as imaginative writers and artists. Piggott concludes that the combined evidence from all available sources leaves modern knowledge of pagan Celtic religion in a "state of the most rudimentary vagueness".

The Reverend William Stukeley (1687–1765) revived a cult of the druids. Stukeley had visited Stonehenge and believed that druidry was the native religion of the British Isles. He laid out a druidical temple in his garden, complete with apple trees and mistletoe. His numerous publications on the Celtic past led to an interest in discovering and recreating a Celtic theology.

Ronald Hutton notes that a number of writers between 1760 and 1840 "set out to 'reconstruct' the principles of a noble and natural religion worthy to be associated with prehistoric philosopher-priests". Of note is Edward Williams (1747–1826) who assumed the name Iolo Morgannwg and "revived" the medieval Order of Bards to teach a "prehistoric system of mystical belief". He added ritual, ceremonies, regalia and hierarchy to texts. The first ritual, the "Gorsedd" (the assembly of new Bards), was held on Primrose Hill in London in 1792. Hutton observes that the notion of a home-grown system of very old wisdom akin to those of the East is very important to many people in the British Isles. This has, he argues, resulted in the belief in the importance of national characteristics, racial identity and folk-memories as a product of the Romantic movement of the late eighteenth century. The Celts have come to represent the

# Sacred mistletoe

Mistletoe is often called the "druid's plant". Godhead is seen to be located in the oak, and the white berries of the mistletoe are thought by some druids to resemble drops of semen. At the druid Winter Solstice ceremony (Alban Arthuan) the mistletoe is ritualistically taken from the oak tree and laid upon an altar. Mistletoe is seen to bring fertility to the earth through its representation of the semen of the oak god given to the earth goddess. Thus fertility is renewed.

*A nineteenth-century romantic portrayal of a druid priestess with sacred mistletoe.*

emotional, mystical, creative and "feminine", while the Anglo-Saxons have been defined as the embodiment of progress, industry, utilitarianism, science and masculinity.

## HISTORICAL EVIDENCE

According to Hutton, the Graeco-Roman writers agreed that the Celtic intellectual elite was divided into bards, druids and vates (only the latter two were religious officials). The druids were more prestigious and were more concerned with philosophy and theology, but according to Julius Caesar they were also teachers, healers and judges. The vates specialized in divination and sacrifice. Hutton points out that the druids were male and that the formal religion of the Celtic peoples was mediated through men, although bards, physicians and women were all depicted as skilled in magic and capable of communing with deities in Irish literature. As far as religious beliefs are concerned, the Graeco-Roman writers tended to agree that the Celts had some sort of theology but it was not recorded

*This painting depicts the druids of Anglesey, North Wales, being massacred by the Romans by order of the governor Suetonius Paulinus. It is conveying a specific nationalistic message and was painted during a Celtic revival by the Scots, Irish and Welsh against English imperialism, and also against the rationalism of the Enlightenment.*

*An arch-druid at the Avebury stone circle in England during the Summer Solstice celebrations. The growing informality of the druid order is shown in the different types of clothing worn.*

in any detail. Most of the early Irish and some of the early Welsh tales described a divine otherworld – a version of the mortal world – where people enjoyed eternal life. This otherworld could be entered via certain doors concealed in mounds, islands, hills, lakes or the sea, and some humans could visit and return.

## THE MODERN INHERITANCE

A great deal is unknown about the religious beliefs of the ancient druids, but modern druids interpret druidism in terms of worshipping the natural forces of the environment through the creative arts. Gone are the days when druidry was represented by men in white robes. Now it attracts a variety of people interested in a Celtic heritage and wanting to relate to nature.

*Druids celebrate the Winter Solstice at Stonehenge. Much controversy and publicity has surrounded the solstice celebrations at Stonehenge. For a number of years rituals were strictly controlled or banned altogether, but at the Summer Solstice in 2000 all restrictions were lifted and many people were able to enjoy being in the midst of the stones as the sun rose over the eastern horizon.*

# THE NEW AGE

The New Age movement originated in 1971 when it emerged in America as a self-conscious form of spirituality. The New Age was originally world-denying in its search for a new order based on spiritual enlightenment. The Earth was seen to be entering a new cycle of evolution marked by a new human consciousness, which would give birth to a new civilization – the "Age of Aquarius" – which would overcome the present corrupt culture by cataclysm and disaster. The idea of a New Age was an amalgamation of various predictions: those of Nostradamus; the American psychic Edgar Cayce; the Theosophical Society; and the Lucis Trust, Rudolf Steiner's anthroposophy. These prophecies were founded in the spiritual traditions of the Maya, Aztec and Hopi people, and also the Judaeo-Christian belief in the second coming of Christ. When the anticipated apocalypse did not arrive there was a "turn inward" and nature became a source of revelation rather than something that obscured real spirit.

*New Age philosophy involves connecting with nature and all its beauty.*

The term "New Age" has become a diffuse term applied to anything from New Age travellers to a particular type of book or music. The New Age is primarily a movement which aims to bring about social change by many and diverse means. By its very nature, according to the sociologist of religion Michael York, it is a term of convergence, one that is more than the sum of its parts, or at least is not to be equated with any one of its parts. According to Marilyn Ferguson there is an "Aquarian conspiracy" – without a political doctrine or a manifesto – which aims to bring about a new form of human consciousness. The Aquarian conspiracy, as advocated by Ferguson, is a new world-view, which has arisen as a response to a crisis. In this vision of a different reality, nature's powers are seen as transformative and a powerful ally, not as a force to be subdued. Ferguson sees human beings as stewards of inner and outer resources, and fundamentally embedded in nature. An expansion of consciousness is required to effect a reunion with all living things, she says: "Just as science demonstrates a web of relationship underlying everything in the universe a glittering network of events, so the mystical experience of

*A holistic perspective – whereby everything in the cosmos is seen to be interrelated – is an underlying theme of the New Age.*

*The Edgar Cayce Foundation, Virginia, USA.*

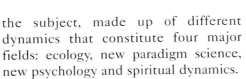

*A New Age group invoke the Earth Spirit at the Merry Maidens stone circle, Cornwall, England.*

*James Lovelock, formulater of the Gaia principle.*

wholeness encompasses all separation".

More recently, the popularization of New Age ideas has been given an immeasurable boost by the publication of James Redfield's *The Celestine Prophecy* in 1994. Combining a new view of science with a conspiracy adventure drama conducted in the rainforests of Peru, Redfield introduces nine "insights" that teach the perennial wisdom that all religions are concerned with humanity creating a relationship with a higher source of divinity. This is a means of stopping the abuse of power and of finding a positive vision of a way to save this planet.

## NEW AGE AND GAIA

For New Agers, the earth is entering a new cycle of evolution marked by a new human consciousness. David Spangler, a leading proponent, describes the New Age as a time of abundance and spiritual enlightenment guided by advanced beings, "perhaps angels or spiritual masters or perhaps emissaries from an extraterrestrial civilization whose spacecraft were the UFOs, [who] would help to create a new civilization". This new cycle of consciousness concerns the invisible and inner dimensions of all life and is, according to William Bloom, a prominent spokesperson and writer on

the subject, made up of different dynamics that constitute four major fields: ecology, new paradigm science, new psychology and spiritual dynamics.

The ecology field draws on the work of the British scientist James Lovelock who, in 1969, proposed the revolutionary principle known as the Gaia hypothesis – that life shapes and controls the environment rather than the other way around. Every individual life form, from

microbe to human, is involved by its own life processes. Earth's atmosphere is actively maintained and regulated by life on the surface for all the species of living beings. Lovelock's work has helped promote a new scientific understanding of life at all levels, from organisms to social systems and ecosystems. It involves a distinct shift in perception from the mechanistic world-view to an encompassing ecological view.

*The New Age is eclectic in its beliefs and practices. Here, a tourist performs the Chinese art of Tai Chi, at the Temple of the Condor, Machu Picchu, Peru. Machu Picchu is said to be the lost city of the Inca, once full of thousands of people as well as various religious shrines and temples.*

*A ceremony involving group dancing at the Findhorn Centre.*

The New Age physicist Fritjof Capra has probably done more than most to popularize New Age science thanks to his critique of mechanistic science, *The Turning Point* (1983), and by his exploration of the parallels between modern physics and eastern religions in *The Tao of Physics* (1976). He calls this change an ecological paradigm. Capra points out that in twentieth-century science a holistic perspective – involving a change in focus from the parts of mechanistic philosophy to the whole, where knowledge is seen as a network of relationships with no firm foundation – has become known as "systems thinking". Systems thinking was pioneered in the early twentieth century by biologists who emphasized the view of living organisms as integrated wholes. It is concerned with context, connections and relationships, and how the essential properties of an organism, or a living system, are properties

*Eileen Caddy, of the Findhorn centre.*

*The meditation room at Findhorn.*

of the whole. Living systems are viewed as part of an interactive web or network.

## FINDHORN

A New Age community in northern Scotland, Findhorn is run according to messages and guidance received from God through Eileen Caddy, one of its founders. It has become a horticultural mecca for communication with nature spirits, devic presences, fairies and other such beings. Eileen Caddy, her husband Peter, and Dorothy MacLean moved to Findhorn in 1962 and established a community of over a hundred members as a centre of light for the Aquarian age. MacLean communicated with devas, which she felt were part of the myriad forms of thought of the divine potential with a vibrant energy that is the very essence of life.

These ideas are influenced by Theosophy, and have been influential in bringing New Age thinking in line with a Christian interpretation of the divine, largely through a focus on the light and communication with angels. The artist and writer Monica Sjöö has launched an attack on such a view, calling the New Age movement patriarchal and fascistic. She claims that New Age embraces reactionary, anti-life views, which are not in tune with the power of women, symbolized as the Goddess. She argues that by creating a God who is all light and transcendent, the rest of creation is demonized. Consequently, the New Age is concerned with a transformation of nature, both internally as healing and a form of development of a higher consciousness, and externally as a relationship with the wider environment. The interconnectedness between all beings, within a network symbolized as Gaia, is very important, and its spiritual aspect is expressed through harmony and light, often within a Christian interpretation.

Healing is an important aspect of the New Age, and complementary or alternative therapies, such as shiatsu, acupressure, reflexology, Reiki and various visualization techniques are very much part of the whole picture.

*New Agers see all life as connected. Here, on a Californian beach, musicians prepare to play music for whales in a ceremony to link humanity with the animals.*

*The Findhorn Foundation, like other New Age groups, communicates with nature spirits, devas, fairies and beings from the otherworld. This painting of a Fairy Tree shows the enchanting world of Faerie.*

# WESTERN SHAMANISM

The central precept of shamanism in the West is regeneration and a revitalization of earth-based "ways of knowing". Inspired by the idea that shamanism is humanity's most ancient and authentic form of spirituality, many modern Western shamanic practitioners turn to what they see as a primordial means of healing and creating connections to nature. Practices include drumming and journeying, as techniques for self-realization and making contact with an otherworldly realm of spirits. Some emphasize the importance of traditions – such as those practised by the Native Americans – others place more importance on finding new ways of engaging with the living world.

*Many modern Western shamanic practitioners attend drumming classes. Drumming helps to induce a trance state for journeying.*

The 1970s saw the emergence of contemporary shamanism, sometimes called neo-shamanism, as a new form of spirituality emanating from the USA. It has been claimed that Mircea Eliade's book *Shamanism: Archaic Techniques of Ecstasy* (1964) was the prototype for the Western shamanism movement, but it took Carlos Castaneda's *The Teachings of Don Juan: A Yaqui Way of Knowledge* (1968), which sold hundreds of thousands of copies, to bring the living experience of an indigenous shamanism to Western culture. This work and nine other books by Castaneda on the same subject are now widely regarded as hoaxes, presenting fiction as fact, but they did popularize shamanism and lead to a fascination with the alternate realities of the shaman.

Shamanism is seen as primordial and authentic by those in the West who are jaded by world religions, particularly Christianity. Native American shamanism, with its circular notion of power and knowledge, symbolized by the medicine wheel, taught about the balance and relationship of all things, and this form of shamanism became particularly fashionable. An alternative to a focus on a particular culture is core shamanism, developed by Michael Harner in his influential book *The Way of the Shaman* (1980). Harner peels off cultural traditions, leaving an essential core, which reveals techniques for changing consciousness during journeying to find power animals, restoring power and

*In earlier centuries, as well as today, shamans have been portrayed in ways that reflect Europeans' fascination with the exotic, and rarely in ways that reflect the shaman's own culture. It is an appalling fact that most shamanic societies have been wiped out by European colonialism and imperialism.*

healing: the essence is in the technique rather than the specific culture. Harner created the Foundation for Shamanic Studies, which has promoted core shamanism techniques through the widespread use of workshops, and now has a number of accredited teachers.

## SHAMANISM IN HISTORY

Traditionally a shaman is a ritual specialist who communicates between different worlds – the ordinary world and the spirit domain – on behalf of his or her people. In the Western, usually urban, context, shamanism may stand for a regeneration and revitalization of ancient Earth-based "ways of knowing" for those who see themselves as dispossessed or alienated from nature as a spiritual source. Westerners can be fascinated with the exotic world of shamanism, but they can also fear it as something that takes them beyond the known.

The West's fascination with shamanism is not new. The historian Gloria Flaherty notes that the curiosity of intellectuals was raised in the fifth century BC when Herodotus reported the death-defying feats of the Scythian soothsaying poets Aristeas and Abaris. She notes that classical scholars throughout the ages have studied Herodotus and have also pointed out numerous other "shamanic" practices of antiquity.

*During the eighteenth and nineteenth centuries, Western Europeans saw shamans as primitives who worshipped evil spirits.*

They have seen in shamanism the origins of theatre, fairy tales and Greek mythology. Flaherty points out that in the eighteenth century there was a good supply of information about shamanism from all over the world, and that by this time certain notions of shamanism had become assimilated into the intellectual mainstream.

Most eighteenth-century observations of shamanism were written from the point of view of interested yet disbelieving western Europeans. Shamanism was viewed in a variety of ways. For some Christian missionaries it was related to native peoples' belief in evil spirits and worship of heathen idols: these "primitives" were thought to have no sense of the true god. For others it concerned a scholarly pursuit of truth into unknown "otherness" and shamanism was subjected to empirical tests and rational analyses. Some attempted to record the activities of vanishing peoples; for others, shamanism epitomized an ageless human activity; while for others there was a fascination with discovering what were seen as the hidden secrets of nature.

The general view of shamanism as an ageless human activity connected with nature has accounted for its rise in popularity in the West. This is the aspect that has led many people to search for a spiritual path in shamanism. According to some Western shamanic practitioners, it is the oldest way in which humanity has sought connection with spirit; it is seen to be an authentic spiritual experience far removed from the dominant religious institutions in the West, which are thought to have lost touch with the experience of spirituality.

### THE MEDICINE WHEEL

Modern Western shamanism offers a series of techniques for self-help and self-realization; it is believed to lead to personal empowerment but also teaches that the individual is part of a broader framework that connects with the rest of the cosmos. The Native American medicine wheel teachings offer a framework for understanding what is, for Westerners, a very different way of seeing the world. The medicine wheel has many meanings and manifestations,

*A modern shamanistic drum showing symbols of the seasons and the zodiac. The drum is an instrument that the shaman can "ride" to take him or her into the spirit otherworld; the symbols relate the shaman to the cosmos.*

*Native American "dream catchers" have become part of popular Western shamanism and the New Age. Adopted from Native American traditions, they are believed to hold on to good dreams and dispel the bad ones.*

ranging from structuring ceremonies and a means for the expression of dreams and visions, to methods for healing. The path of personal transformation on the medicine wheel is said to take the knower and the known through a spiral of experiences that link the individual, and his or her own course from birth to death, with the seasons and the wider whole.

The teachings of Sun Bear, who is of Chippewa descent, are based on his vision of the medicine wheel and incorporate elements from various Native American cultures. The wheel revolves around a Creator Stone, which is the centre of all life and radiates energy to the rest of the wheel. Seven stones surrounding the Creator form the centre circle, the foundation of all life. They are, in sunwise direction: Earth Mother, Father Sun, Grandmother Moon, Turtle clan, Frog clan, Thunderbird clan and Butterfly clan. Four stones mark the outer circle, and these are the Spirit Keepers: Waboose in the north, Wabun in the east, Shawnodese in the south and

Mudjekeewis in the west. From the Spirit Keeper stones radiate qualities – such as cleansing, renewal, purity, clarity and wisdom – that are necessary to gain the sacred space of the Creator in the centre of the circle. Between the four Spirit Keeper stones are the 12 moon stones of the outer circle.

Issues of cultural appropriation or, in other words, the stealing of an oppressed people's spiritual heritage by the descendents of Western colonialism, are slowly infiltrating popular books and journals aimed at those interested in practising shamanism in the West. There is a move to search for Western "indigenous" versions, and a whole range of shamanisms – from Celtic to Wiccan – are being "rediscovered". Weekend workshops and drumming circles, where participants can journey in trance to find their spirit guides, are becoming more and more popular.

Healing is often a central component of much of this work, and shamanic

*Soul journeying is an important part of modern Western shamanic practice.*

practitioners journey to retrieve lost soul parts – for themselves and for others – on a regular basis. The essence of shamanic healing concerns the spiritual removal of aspects of a person that should not be

there, and returning those spiritual parts that should. This is often done with the aid of spirit beings sometimes called power animals, or totems.

However, shamanic practitioners are not the same thing as shamans: a shamanic training does not make a shaman. For Gordon MacLellan, who is a contemporary Western shaman working in environmental education, being a shaman is a practical job of mediating between the human world and the world of spirits. Seeing the role of the shaman in modern Britain as one of communicator and "patterner" with nature, he says that a modern shaman has to find new ways of engaging humans with the living world. Shamans work with communities and draw their inspiration from the Otherworld, which is an abode of spirits where we "meet the talking foxes and watch the shapes of the stone people unfold from the rocks on a hillside … This is the shaman's world. The shaman moves through an Otherworld that may

*The medicine wheel of the Native American shaman has many meanings. It acts as an object of contemplation that links the individual into a wider sacred whole. Here a man is meditating before a medicine wheel at Sedona, Arizona, USA.*

# Shamanic tools

Smudge sticks and smudge fans are used to cleanse the body, mind and surroundings before a spirit journey is commenced, or simply as a way to clear the mind and purify the body. A smudge stick is lit and the fragrant smoke that comes from it is directed to the appropriate place by the fan. Smudge sticks are often made from white sage, but also from other sweet smelling herbs that have particular significance or cleansing qualities. Rattles are sometimes used instead of a drum to help a shaman go into a trance; they can also be used during a healing to call spirits, diagnose illness and open a person to the spirits.

*A smudge fan made from feathers.*

*A rattle made from dried seed pods.*

*White sage smudge sticks for cleansing.*

correspond exactly with the territory she calls home but here is midnight and a world frosted with energy like ice on every leaf, where the mist at dawn is a swirling, pouring cloud of spirals spilling out of damp hollows." The Otherworld is not other at all, it is also this world.

Not tapping directly into an extant tradition, and gaining inspiration from a number of sources, Gordon MacLellan claims that some of the most exciting ceremonies have grown with grass roots environmental action: "Whole rituals take shape through the need of people to draw upon their own energy, to recognize their strength and to acknowledge the land and their feelings for it that can bring them to battle on its behalf." MacLellan feels that these rituals represent a growth that breaks traditions, bridges class, belief and age distinction, and suggests that these eco-warriors are the latest practitioners of a particular magic of the modern age, and the inheritors of shamanic traditions.

*Gordon MacLellan, a modern Western shaman.*

*Western shamanism today is often concerned with healing, and here Jo Crow, a Western shaman, drums herself into a trance during a ceremony.*

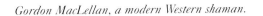

# THE NORTHERN TRADITION

Heathens, or practitioners of the Northern tradition of magic, attempt to recapture an ancient Indo-European way of life through the mythology of Odin and other Scandanavian gods and goddesses. Northern cosmology is focused on the world tree Yggdrasil, the connecting point of nine worlds, at the bottom of which sit the three sister Norns who weave a web of fate called the "wyrd". This is a very specialized tradition and one which, unlike the Western Mysteries, does not take strands of belief from other traditions. The spiritual path that practitioners of the Northern tradition follow looks to the Icelandic Sagas for inspiration in matters concerning human dilemmas and conflicts.

*Odin the Norse god with his two crows Huginn (Thought) and Muninn (Memory).*

While many modern pagans claim Celtic origins for their practice, some are drawn to the traditions and history of Germanic, Scandinavian or Anglo-Saxon peoples, the spiritual beliefs that are said to be indigenous to northern Europe.

Comprising Germanic, Baltic, Norse and Celtic strands, these beliefs relate to areas of Germany, the Baltic countries of northern Poland and western Russia, Iceland, Scandinavia, Austria, the Czech Republic, Switzerland, northern France, Ireland and Britain and are collectively described as the "Northern tradition". Often preferring to call themselves heathens, practitioners of the Northern tradition attempt to recapture and reconstruct what they see as the ancient Nordic tribal religion, mainly through the lore and the sagas as outlined in twelfth- and thirteenth-century literature, especially that of the Icelander Snorri Sturluson (1179–1241). Seeing their beliefs as part of an ancient Indo-European way of life, practitioners of Northern magic create a different spiritual path to those who follow the Western Mystery tradition with its focus on Egyptian and Judaeo-Christian mythology.

While most practitioners of the Northern tradition see their magical practices as part of a rich variety of spiritual paths and welcome all interested seekers, it is unfortunate that in the past this form of magical organization has

*The goddess Freyja, mistress of magic and witchcraft. She is said to own a falcon skin that enables her to fly to the underworld. She is depicted here flying with swans.*

attracted a minority who have neo-Nazi sympathies. A tendency to nationalism by some in the Northern tradition in Britain has led to tensions with other pagan or magical groups, but now the general consensus among most heathens is that they will not hold with any form of racism or nationalism.

## TROTH TO THE GODS

The main Northern tradition is known as "Odinism" or "Ásatrú": "loyalty or troth to the gods", or "allegiance to the deities". The principle god is called Odin in Scandinavian, Wotan in German and Woden in Anglo-Saxon. Odin is associated with inspiration, writing, combat and the dead. He has one eye, wears a wide-brimmed hat and often a blue cloak, and carries a magical spear. Two ravens, Huginn (Thought) and Muninn (Memory) sit on his shoulders, birds of battle and also symbols of flights to find wisdom.

Although the goddesses are equal with the gods in Northern mythology, little is known about them. For example, there is not much information on Odin's partner, the goddess Frigg, who is Queen of the Heavens. There were 12 gods and 13 goddesses in the Norse pantheon, and these included the fertility god Freyr and his sister Freyja, who is associated with war and rides to battle in a chariot drawn by two cats. Freyja is mistress of magic and witchcraft, and owns a falcon skin, which enables her to take falcon form on journeys to the underworld. The god Thor is the son of Odin and the Earth, is second in importance to Odin and represents order, law and stability. Loki, the son of two giants and the foster-brother of Odin, is a trickster figure who embodies all that is dark, unpredictable, and ambiguous. Loki is necessary as a catalyst to create change, without which no movement could take place.

Northern cosmology is centred on the world tree Yggdrasil, which is the connecting point of nine worlds; each world is populated by one race or type of being, such as giants, dwarves, elves, deities and humans. In Norse mythology, the Norns are three sisters who sit

*A twelfth-century Viking tapestry depicting Odin on the left carrying an axe, with a representation of the cosmic tree Yggdrasil, from which he hung. In the centre is the god Thor carrying a hammer, and on the right is the fertility god Freyr holding an ear of corn.*

at the base of Yggdrasil and spin a web of fate called "wyrd". The past and future are not seen as separate, and the future is seen to be in the present; time is not viewed as a linear progression and wyrd can be changed to some degree. The amount of influence that it is possible to exert on wyrd has been likened to sailing by the psychologist Brian Bates, who is the author of two popular books on the subject. According to him, a skilled magical practitioner is like a sailor who has the ability to trim the sails in order to change or adjust direction but cannot alter the overall course of the

*The Norse tradition was depicted in heroic, Romantic terms by a variety of artists, as in this nineteenth-century painting by Hans Gabriel Jentzsch showing a Winter Solstice festival honouring the onset of winter.*

current. According to Ronald Hutton, there is not enough information to make comparisons between the cults of the Celts, Romans, Greeks and Eastern peoples and those of the Germanic and Norse peoples, but wyrd, the idea of an overwhelming web of destiny that shapes the whole world, appears to be a significant northern characteristic.

Since 1973, Ásatrú has been one of the officially recognized religions of Iceland, and while it has not reached that status in other countries it is growing in popularity. Northern tradition groups in Britain are the Odinic Rite, Odinshof, Hammarens Ordens Sällskap and the Rune Gild. In America the Ásatrú Alliance, the Ásatrú Folk Assembly, the Odinist Fellowship, the Ring of Troth and the Rune Gild are prominent. Some heathens celebrate the eight pagan seasonal festivals and lunar cycles, but others dismiss these as of

*A modern heathen celebration of May Day in Navan, Northern Ireland.*

recent origin and observe what they see as more authentic Northern European rites of Winternights, Yule and Sigrblot. Winternights is the celebration of the onset of winter, harvest festival and an honouring of the dead; Yule is the observance of the longest night and New Year, a time of oaths and fateful encounters with otherworldly visitors such as the dead and divinities. Sigrblot is a victory celebration of the beginning of summer – of vitality over winter gloom or a celebration of coming victories in trading or raiding.

The runes are used as a divination system in the Northern tradition. Divination was important to the Germanic

peoples, and according to the Roman writer Tacitus, they paid much attention to the "casting of lots":

*Their method of casting lots is a simple one: they cut a branch from a fruit-bearing tree and divide it into small pieces, which they mark with certain distinctive signs and scatter at random onto a white cloth. Then the priest of the community, if the lots are consulted publicly, or the father of the family, if it is done privately, after invoking the gods with eyes raised to heaven, picks up three pieces, one at a time, and interprets them according to the signs previously marked upon them.*

*A modern heathen celebration of midsummer or Sigrblot, the victory of summer over winter. People join hands around a decked pole to celebrate the return of the sun.*

*A ninth-century casket with runic inscriptions.*

*Rune stones in Gørlev church, Zealand, Denmark, from the tenth or eleventh century.*

The true nature of the runes is said to have been revealed to Odin as he hung upon the world tree Yggdrasil for nine days and nine nights. Odin's account is recorded in the Håvamål:

*I know that I hung on the*
*windswept tree*
*For nine days and nine nights,*
*Wounded by a spear,*
*And given to Odin,*
*Myself to myself,*
*On that tree*
*Which no man knows*
*From what roots it grows,*
*They gave me no bread*
*Nor drinking horn.*
*I looked down,*
*I picked up the runes,*
*Screaming, I took them.*
*Then I fell back.*

Heathens, like practitioners of magic in other traditions, seek to live in contact with the "spirit of place", seeing their gods as unique entities and as part of the all-embracing web of wyrd.

*A set of runes used for divination.*

# Table of Runes:

Today, modern magicians of the Northern tradition use the runes as a system of sacred knowledge and expression of eternal universal laws; like the tarot, they represent the deeper mysteries in symbolic form. The Elder Futhark is an alphabet of 24 runes or staves, and there are many variations of this basic pattern: some have more characters, like the Anglo-Saxon variant with 29, and others have less, like the Scandinavian version that has 16.

| LETTER | SIGN | NAME | MEANING |
| --- | --- | --- | --- |
| F | ᚠ | Feoh | Cattle |
| U | ᚢ | Ur | Auroch |
| TH | ᚦ | Thorn | Thorn |
| A | ᚨ | Ansur | A mouth |
| R | ᚱ | Rad | A cartwheel |
| K | ᚲ | Ken | A torch |
| G | ᚷ | Geofu | A gift |
| W | ᚹ | Wynn | Happiness |
| H | ᚺ | Hagall | Hail |
| N | ᚾ | Nied | Need |
| I | ᛁ | Is | Ice |
| J | ᛃ | Jara | Harvest |
| Y | ᛇ | Eoh | A yew tree |
| P | ᛈ | Peorth | A dice cup |
| Z | ᛉ | Elhaz | An elk |
| S | ᛋ | Sigel | The sun |
| T | ᛏ | Tyr | The god Tyr |
| B | ᛒ | Beorc | A birch tree |
| E | ᛖ | Ehwaz | A horse |
| M | ᛗ | Mann | A human |
| L | ᛚ | Lagu | Water, sea |
| NG | ᛜ | Ing | The god Ing |
| D | ᛞ | Daeg | Day (light) |
| O | ᛟ | Othel | A possession |

# SATANISM

For Satanists, Satan or the Devil is symbolic of a hidden force in nature responsible for the workings of earthly affairs and representing the spirit of inspiration and human progress. Revolting against organized religion – which is only suitable for "the herd" – Satanists allegedly seek to harness what have been called dark forces to liberate the will in the advancement of evolution. Claims that Satanists conduct rituals to abuse children are reminiscent of early modern witchcraft accusations, and are vigorously denied. Satanism concerns the self-affirmation and freedom of the individual.

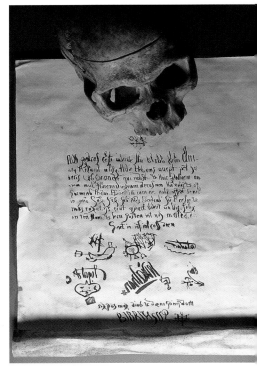

*A pact supposedly signed by demons in looking-glass Latin, and used in evidence at the witchcraft trial of Urbain Grandier in 1634. The reversed signatures of Satanas, Beelzebub, Lucifer, Leviathan and Astararoth may be seen.*

The Christian division of the world into light and dark or good and evil, the battlelines drawn between the God of good against demonic forces of evil headed by the Devil or Satan, has been a positive invitation to some to join the dark side. Anton Szandor La Vey, the founder of the Church of Satan, has taken this position one step further by formulating a religion based on worshipping the dark forces. La Vey was a great showman and played to his audience by dressing up as the Devil but, in his view, the Devil was not a deity that represented the opposite of God but a hidden force in nature responsible for the workings of earthly affairs. The Devil represented the spirit of progress and inspiraton for the advancement of human beings, as well as the spirit of revolt that leads to freedom from organized religions like Christianity, which are only suitable for the "herd".

On Spring Equinox or Walpurgisnacht, 30 April 1966, Anton La Vey shaved his head and declared the beginning of the Age of Satan. This marked the start of a number of Church of Satan workshops, seminars, and rituals that were open to the public and conducted at his home, the "Black House". This was the first church of its type, but it was not the first group that had met to honour Satan. In England in the eighteenth century, Sir Francis Dashwood had formed the Hellfire Club, and Rabelais' fictional utopia, the "Abbey of Thelema", had inspired Aleister Crowley to found his version in Sicily in 1920, with the motto "Fait ce que voudras" ("Do what thou wilt").

## ANTON LA VEY

La Vey was born in Chicago on 11 April 1930, and was allegedly taught legends of vampires and witches by his gypsy grandmother, who passed on to him the folklore of her native Transylvania. Dropping out of school because it was boring, La Vey joined the Clyde Beatty Circus as a cage boy, watering and feeding lions and tigers. He became an assistant trainer and also played the organ. Later he joined a carnival and it

*Sir Francis Dashwood (1708–81), pictured seated, formed a Satanist group called the Hellfire Club in the eighteenth century.*

*A fictional utopia, invented by François Rabelais (1494–1553) inspired the magician Aleister Crowley to found his own version of utopia in the early twentieth century.*

was stopped and Church of Satan activities were carried out in Satanic grottos in several countries. La Vey's stated goal was the creation of a police state in which the weak were weeded out and an achievement-oriented leadership was permitted to pursue the mysteries of black magic.

The Satanic Bible is a book that outlines the theory and ritual practice of Satanic magic. Magic is separated into lesser, everyday magic, such as that used for psychological manipulation and tricks to get people to do what the Satanist wants, and greater or ceremonial magic. Satanic rituals, according to La Vey, do not involve the sacrifice of animals or babies; they do not involve a negative reversal of Christian ritual – as in the

*Below: Anton Szandor La Vey, the founder of the modern Church of Satan, has followed in the satanic tradition of Dashwood and Crowley in liberating the individual will from the fetters of organized religion. He is shown here on the left with "Satania" lying on an altar and "Hellas" and his wife "Elysia" (on the right) looking on.*

*Above: Satan is seen as an arch-rebel and individualist by modern Satanists and in Blake's portrayal of him rousing the rebel angels.*

was here that he learnt hypnosis and studied the occult as assistant to a magician. During a period when he worked as a photographer for the San Francisco Police Department he saw the worst side of humanity, and came to detest the sanctimonious attitude of people who saw in human violence the work of God's will. He left the Police Department to play the organ in nightclubs and theatres.

In the 1950s La Vey started gaining a reputation for black magic in San Francisco and formed a group called the Order of Trapezoid, which later evolved into the governing body of the Church of Satan. It espoused a down-to-earth philosophy with an emphasis on the "carnal, lustful, natural instincts of man" without guilt or sin. Its methods sought to harness the dark forces to change situations according to will. His publicity stunts included baptizing his own three-year-old daughter Zeena in 1967, dedicating her to the Devil. The following year he played the part of the Devil in the film *Rosemary's Baby*. In 1972 the public work at the Black House

# The Nine Satanic Principles

1  Satan represents indulgence, instead of abstinence!

2  Satan represents vital existence, instead of spiritual pipe dreams!

3  Satan represents undefiled wisdom, instead of hypocritical self-deceit!

4  Satan represents kindness to those who deserve it, instead of love wasted on ingrates!

5  Satan represents vengeance, instead of turning the other cheek!

6  Satan represents responsibility to the responsible, instead of concern for psychic vampires!

7  Satan represents man as just another animal, sometimes better, more often worse than those that walk on all-fours, who, because of his divine spiritual and intellectual developmenti, has become the most vicious animal of all!

8  Satan represents all of the so-called sins, as they all lead to physical, mental, or emotional gratification!

9  Satan has been the best friend the Church has ever had, as he has kept it in business all these years!

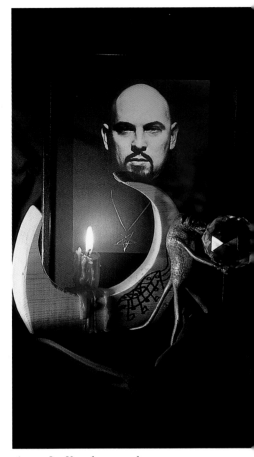

*Anton La Vey, the great showman.*

popular stereotype of a black mass conducted by a defrocked priest worshipping a naked woman on an altar – but allegedly concern celebration and purges from sin. A Satanic wedding, for example, consecrates the joys of the flesh with a lust rite. La Vey outlines nine Satanic principles (see box above), on which his church is run.

The Satanic Church attracted an international following and at its peak it was said to have about 25,000 members (although this claim was probably greatly exaggerated). It has included celebrities among its number; the best-known was the actress Jayne Mansfield, who was killed in a car accident that was allegedly foreseen by La Vey.

### THE TEMPLE OF SET

By the mid-1980s another Satanic organization, called the Temple of Set and also based in San Francisco, had attracted several hundred members. It was founded by Michael A. Aquino (a lieutenant-colonel of the US Army Reserve), Lilith Sinclair and Betty Ford (not the First Lady of that name) and is a society based on the worship of the Egyptian god Set or Seth, who is viewed as the forerunner of Satan. The Temple

of Set is an initiatory society that is interested in people of high intelligence and the advancement of genetic evolution. Aquino prophesied an apocalypse in which only the members of the Temple of Set, as the elect, would survive. There are many who are attracted to Satanic activities – the frisson of being

a part of an organization that is seen by Christians as the very essence of evil is compelling to some.

### SATANIC RITUAL ABUSE

In the late 1980s a moral panic about Satanism that took the form of ritual abuse led to scores of children being taken into care in Britain. The panic started in 1988 in the USA, when allegations of Satanic ritual abuse were made by social workers, and these ideas were passed on to their British counterparts at an international conference. Satanic abuse was seen to involve extreme acts of human sacrifice, cannibalism and the sexual abuse of children in orgiastic rituals, the purpose of which was an act of Devil-worship or witchcraft.

These allegations, which are strikingly similar to those levelled at witches during the early modern witch hunts, were fuelled by evangelical Christian groups.

*Jayne Mansfield, the Hollywood actress, was a member of La Vey's Satanic Church.*

*The work of Aleister Crowley has been an inspiration to many Satanists. This seal was designed by him and depicts an inverted pentagram, or five-pointed star, a symbol now used by Satanists.*

*Satanism and witchcraft bring up people's deepest fears. Here a woman is portrayed as the Devil, and combines femaleness and evil in a manner common to the early modern stereotype of the witch.*

"Satanic" activities, from the use of masks and costumes to the invocation of supernatural powers.

In 1994 the British government ordered a report to investigate the abuse. Eighty-four cases of alleged ritual abuse were investigated. Three did show evidence of ritual used to entrap the children by claims of mystical powers, or to prevent them from telling, but none were considered Satanic. In other words, the motivation for the abuse was sexual rather than Satanic. The report was critical of the interviewing techniques of the social services, saying that interviewers had employed leading questions, and used repeated questions. The report said that the children had told the adults what they thought they wanted to hear. This last aspect is reminiscent of the early modern European witch trials in which confessions were extracted to conform to the judge's views of diabolic witchcraft.

Satanism, like witchcraft, tends to bring up peoples' deepest fears. Undoubtedly there are individuals who perform immoral acts – but this does not justify the tendency that society has of branding a whole system of belief on the basis of conjecture and unproven rumour, a lesson that should have been learned from the times of the European witch hunts.

These groups offer counselling to people trying to sever their links with the occult. They claim that an interest in the occult starts people off on the slippery slope towards Satanism, and that people are recruited via New Age fairs and international Satanic organizations. At the time of the allegations, newspaper stories of survivors of Satanic abuse and confessions of former Satanists – who told about young girls being used as "brood mares" by being made pregnant and then forced to have abortions at five months so that the foetuses could be used in sacrifice – added to the panic.

In Britain, the social services and the charity the National Society for the Prevention of Cruelty to Children organized a survey of social workers, and the results reported a wide range of

*Charles Manson as he appeared in court in California, accused of Satanic murder.*

# CHAOS MAGIC

Unlike most other magical practices chaos magic is not a spiritual path. Using the maxim "Nothing is true, everything is permitted", chaos magicians emphasize pragmatic techniques and observable results in the world as it is directly experienced as a form of sorcery. The aim is to achieve alternative states of consciousness or "gnosis". Chaos magic has acquired a certain notoriety for being sinister, even Satanic. This is because it rejects spiritual elements in its practices. Above all, it offers an opportunity to explore non-ordinary reality without the hindrance of accepted beliefs, and in the process, its practitioners claim, inspiration, knowledge, power and heightened perception are gained.

Chaos magic was created in the late 1970s with the emergence of punk rock and the theoretical explorations in science that came to be called chaos theory. Influenced by both Aleister Crowley and Austin Osman Spare, chaos magic is above all a practical approach to practising magic. Chaos magicans claim that all the methods of working magic are the same, despite differing symbols and belief systems. Chaos magic is thus a means to an end, rather than an end in itself. It claims to eschew the dogma of other approaches in its emphasis on avoiding the use of any one magical "system", advocating experimentation

*The Great Cthulhu, lord of dreams, telepathy and madness, is an entity with octopoid head and wings and is based on the work of the science fiction writer Howard Phillips Lovecraft.*

*Austin Osman Spare, artist and occultist, and source of inspiration to chaos magicians.*

*Chaos magic came into being at the same time as punk rock, a movement that was epitomized by the band the Sex Pistols.*

with many practices. According to chaos magician Phil Hine, chaos magic is concerned with deconditioning from "the mesh of beliefs, attitudes and fictions about self, society and the world". Through the idea of the "paradigm" (which in chaos magic means the individual taking up a personal, magical role model), the magician can switch into and out of many magical techniques using the maxim. "If it works, use it", while leaving his or her beliefs behind. Chaos is not a religion – its focus is not on what may be termed "spirituality" – it is more specifically the utilization of magical techniques for the attainment of alternate states of consciousness or "gnosis". "Spiritual truth" has no meaning; whatever feels right is important. It glorifies fantasy and is a conscious and deliberate dislocation from any historical and spiritual tradition.

## Basic Principles

The basic principles of chaos magic are expressed by the maxim "Nothing is true, everything is permitted". They may be summed up as: an avoidance of any form of dogmatism; a focus on personal experience; technical excellence in development of skills and abilities in the performance of a magical act; deconditioning the self by modifying and discarding beliefs and "ego-fictions"; and an eclectic and diverse approach, choosing from themes as wide apart as science fiction or tantrism, or adopting the beliefs of a spiritual system, if they are thought to serve a useful function. The overall aim is to achieve gnosis as a form of inner knowledge.

Eight forms of magic are represented on the "chaosphere". Octarine is pure or raw magic, representing the development of theories and philosophies. Black magic is death magic and concerns the ritual rehearsal of death. Blue magic is concerned with the control of other people and the creation of wealth. Red magic is associated with war. Yellow magic is involved with the ego or self-image. Green magic is about love. Orange magic concerns thought and living by the wits. Purple or silver is associated with sex magic.

*The chaos magician Phil Hine holding a chaosphere-headed staff.*

Peter Carroll, in his book *Liber Kaos* (1992), sees magic as a consequence of the structure of the universe, and he visualizes it as five serpents – of space, time, mass, energy and aether – each biting their tails and giving birth to themselves out of their own mouths. Carroll's view of the universe indicates that it is random, as is the individual's relationship with it: he offers no permanent model. His early writings appeared in the magazine *The New Equinox*, and it was here that the magical order the Illuminates of Thanateros (IOT) was first advertised. The IOT was formed in 1978 by Peter Carroll and Ray Sherwin to provide inspiration for chaos magicians. It was not a teaching order with initiated hierarchies but rather an organization where people could come together to practise and publish practical magic. This was not as easy as it sounds, some people expected teaching and leaders, but no rules or instructions were ever given, only suggestions on how to reach "that which could not be taught".

*A chaos magic altar demonstrating its eclectic nature: Baphomet sits in the centre surrounded by a skull mala, a glass thunderbolt, a green baboon fetish, a lizard fetish, a crystal with a demon inside, a damaru, and a three-dimensional chaosphere in the bottom right hand corner.*

## THE THANATEROS RITUAL

Phil Hine, writing in *Condensed Chaos* (1995), describes magic as "a doorway through which we step into mystery, wildness and immanence", and ritual is one way of achieving this. For chaos magicians there is no one shared reality when ritual workings are conducted, but rituals are seen to create opportunities for experiencing a magical state of consciousness. Before any magical work is undertaken a "banishing ritual" is performed. This is a preparation and centring exercise, which allows the magician to focus on the task ahead rather than on more mundane thoughts, and it also is supposed to clear the ritual space from unwanted atmospheres. Banishing rituals typically have three parts. The first section focuses awareness on the magician and is aimed at clearing the mind of unwanted thoughts by the visualization of white light being drawn through the body. The second creates a symbolic universe with the magician at the centre. The following is a suggestion by Phil Hine, and may be done by focusing on the eight rays of magic of the chaosphere and declaring:

> *These are my weapons*
> *Expressions of my will*
> *I grasp them lightly*
> *I stand poised, at the centre*
> *The Universe dances for my pleasure.*

The third section involves an identification of the chosen source of inspiration.

The Thanateros ritual is an example of a "celebration of Chaoist principles" according to Peter Carroll, and it concerns the invocation of the power of chaos. The magician tricks his or her consciousness into an ecstatic magical state by what is called the "neither-neither" effect. By meditating on the death of self in the act of sex, and the birth of self in an encounter with death, the ritual simulates encounters with both sex and death, and then with both of these experiences simultaneously, which is said to force conception beyond its normal limits. After a statement of intent and litanies, Eros and Thanatos are invoked:

*The chaos Thanateros ritual is a process that simulates an encounter with sex and death – in the death of self in the act of sex, and the birth of self in an encounter with death. This is a nineteenth-century painting of Thanatos (Greek god of death) depicting aspects of sex and death.*

> *Invocation to Eros:*
> *So come Eros, we invoke thee*
> *You who created us*
> *In the chaotic conjunction*
> *Of genetic roulette*
> *Come create us anew*
> *And kill us again!*
> *Our lovers approach*
> *Our breathing quickens*
> *As they come closer*
> *Our breathing quickens*
> *As we are clasped together*
> *Our breathing quickens*
> *At the thrill of touch*
> *Our breathing quickens*
> *We begin to gasp*
> *We are ready to surrender*
> *Three, Two, One,*
> *(Cry of Climax)!*

> *Invocation to Thanatos:*
> *So come Thanatos, we invoke thee*
> *We accept your bargain*
> *Come kill us again*
> *And create us anew*
> *Our nemesis approaches*
> *Grinning skull and upraised scythe*

> *Our breathing quickens*
> *Closer it comes and closer*
> *Our breathing quickens*
> *Death stares us in the face*
> *Our breathing quickens*
> *Upraised terrible scythe*
> *We begin to gasp*
> *When it falls we shall die*
> *Three, Two, One,*
> *(Cry of Death Terror)!*

The ritual finishes with ecstatic laughter as an expression of the neither-neither: the energy being raised is either used for itself or to cast a spell.

## THE CTHULHU MYTHOS

Another way of working with chaos magic is with what is known as the Cthulhu Mythos. Cthulhu, high priest of the "Great Old Ones", created by science fiction writer Howard Phillips Lovecraft (1890–1937), is a zoomorphic entity with an octopoid head and wings. Contact with him is said to unite the chthonic roots of primeval consciousness to the stellar magicks of the future. Phil Hine writes, in *The Pseudonomicon*, that the Old Ones, who are alien to human civilization and rationality, have a close relationship with wild places – particularly stone circles and "strange manifestations" – and have been cast forth from the earth and forgotten by civilized humanity and its materialistic vision. They are ever-present, "lurking at the frontiers of order, in places where the wild power of nature can be felt". They are chaotic, as Nature is chaotic, and they retain their primal power since they cannot be explained.

The Old Ones manifest into the everyday world through gateways in wild, lonely places entangled with local myth and folklore; associated with strange lights, subterranean noises, stone circles, ancient ruins, strange angles, tunnels, wells and the gates of "dreaming, trance and madness". A core feature of the Cthulhu Mythos is said to be transformation into a new mode of being. After initiation by fear and near madness that shatters the old conception of self, and by dreaming and astral visions, the magician reaches a form of consciousness that is more tenuous and chaotic than ordinary reality.

Masks are an important part of magical work: they ease the identification with otherworldly beings and the loss of a sense of the self. This is a spirit of Chaos mask.

*A statue of Baphomet, who is popular with chaos magicians, displaying hermaphroditic qualities.*

# Tantric Altar

Chaos magic takes an eclectic approach to magic, and may utilize other magicial traditions. Altars are ideal for demonstrating this, as the symbolism and connections can be so diverse. Here, on this Chaos Tantric altar, is a selection of items that takes in several different traditions. It includes a yoni lingam (top right), a small statue of Kali, goddess of death and destruction (top left), a damaru, a thunderbolt (bottom right), and a Tibetan phurba or ritual knife (bottom left) used for "nailing demons". The altar contains eight bowls of water for the eight directions and is surrounded by a skull mala.

*A Chaos Tantric altar.*

91

# BIBLIOGRAPHY

Ankarloo, B. and Clark, S. *Witchcraft and Magic in Europe: Ancient Greece and Rome.* Philadelphia: University of Pennsylvania Press, 1999.

Ankarloo, B. and Henningsen, G., eds. *Early Modern European Witchcraft: Centres and Peripheries.* Oxford: Clarendon, 1993.

Arrowsmith, N. *A Field Guide to the Little People.* London: Pan, 1977.

Aswyn, F. *Northern Mysteries and Magick: Runes, Gods and Feminine Powers.* St Paul, MN: Llewellyn, 1998.

Baring, A. and Cashford, J. *The Myth of the Goddess.* London: Arkana, 1993.

Bates, B. *The Way of Wyrd.* London: Arrow, 1983.

Bates, B. *The Wisdom of Wyrd.* London: Rider, 1996.

Burton Russell, G. *The historical Satan.* In: J.T. Richardson, J. Best and D. Bromley, eds. *The Satanism Scare.* New York: Aldine de Gruyter, 1991.

Capra, F. *The Tao of Physics.* London: Flamingo, 1976.

Capra, F. *The Turning Point.* London: Flamingo, 1983.

Cardozo, A.R. *A modern American witch-craze.* In: M. Marwick, ed. *Witchcraft and Sorcery.* London: Penguin, 1990.

Carr-Gomm, P. *The Druid Tradition.* Shaftesbury, Dorset: Element, 1995.

Carroll, P. *Liber Null and Psychonaut.* York Beach, ME: Samuel Weiser, 1987.

Clark, E.E. *Indian Legends of the Pacific Northwest.* Berkeley and Los Angeles: University of California Press, 1953.

Clark, S. *Thinking with Demons.* Oxford: Clarendon, 1999.

Cohn, N. *Europe's Inner Demons: the Demonization of Christians in Medieval Christendom.* London: Pimlico, 1993.

Crowley, V. *Wicca: the Old Religion in the New Age.* Wellingborough: Aquarian, 1989.

Cunliffe, B. *The Celtic World.* London: Constable, 1992.

Cunliffe, B. *Prehistoric Europe: an Illustrated Guide.* Oxford: Open University Press, 1997.

Douglas, A. *The Tarot.* London: Penguin, 1974.

Eliade, M. *Shamanism.* Princeton: Princeton University Press, 1974.

Eliade, M. *Some observations on European witchcraft.* In: *History of Religions,* 14, pp. 149–72, 1975.

Farrar, S. and Farrar, J. *A Witches' Bible Compleat.* New York: Magickal Childe, 1991.

Gardner, G. *Witchcraft Today.* New York: Magickal Childe, 1988.

Gijswijt-Hofstra, M., Levack, B. and Porter, R., eds. *History of Witchcraft and Magic in Europe: the Eighteenth and Nineteenth Centuries.* London: Athlone Press, 1999.

Godbeer, R. *The Devil's Dominion.* Cambridge: Syndicate, 1992.

Graves, R. *The Greek Myths.* London: Penguin, 1960.

Graves, R. *The White Goddess.* London: Faber & Faber, 1981.

Greenwood, S. *Magic, Witchcraft and the Otherworld.* Oxford: Berg, 2000.

Harvey, G. *Listening People, Speaking Earth.* London: Hurst & Co, 1997.

Hill, F. *A Delusion of Satan: The Full Story of the Salem Witch Trials.* London: Hamish Hamilton, 1996.

Hine, P. *Condensed Chaos.* Arizona: New Falcon Publications, 1995.

Hine, P. *Prime Chaos.* Arizona: New Falcon Publications, 1999.

Hutton, R. *The Pagan Religions of the Ancient British Isles.* London: BCA, 1991.

Hutton, R. *The roots of modern paganism.* In: G. Harvey and C. Hardman, eds. *Paganism Today.* London: Thorsons, 1996.

Hutton, R. *The Triumph of the Moon.* Oxford: Oxford University Press, 1999.

James, S. *The Atlantic Celts: Ancient People or Modern Invention?* London: British Museum Press, 1999.

Jones, P. and Pennick, N. *A History of Pagan Europe.* London: Routledge, 1995.

Katz, R. *Boiling Energy: Community Healing among the Kalahari Kung.* Cambridge, MA: Harvard University Press, 1982.

Kelly, A. *Crafting the Art of Magic: a History of Modern Witchcraft 1939 1964.* St Paul, MN: Llewellyn, 1991.

King, F. *Magic: the Western Tradition.* London: Thames & Hudson, 1975.

King, F. *Modern Ritual Magic.* Bridport, Dorset: Prism, 1990.

Klaniczay, G. *Hungary: The Accusations and the Universe of Popular Magic.* In: B. Ankarloo and G. Henningsen, eds. *Early modern European Witchcraft: Centres and Peripheries.* Oxford: Clarendon, 1993.

Knappert, J. *African Mythology.* London: Diamond, 1995.

La Vey, A. *The Satanic Bible.* New York: Avon Books, 1969.

Larner, C. *Enemies of God.* London: Chatto & Windus, 1981.

Levack, B. *The Witch-Hunt in Early Modern Europe.* London: Longman, 1995.

Lévi-Strauss, C. *The effectiveness of symbols.* In: W. Lessa and E. Vogt eds. *Reader in Comparative Religion: an Anthropological Approach.* New York: Harper & Row, 1979.

Low, M. *Celtic Christianity and Nature: Early Irish and Hebridean Traditions.* Edinburgh: Polygon, 1999.

Luce, J. *The End of Atlantis.* London: BCA, 1973.

Luhrmann, T. *Persuasions of the Witch's Craft.* Oxford: Blackwell, 1989.

Macfarlane, A. *Witchcraft in Tudor and Stuart England: a Regional and Comparative Study.* London: Routledge, 1999.

MacLellan, G. *Dancing on the edge: shamanism in modern Britain*. In: G. Harvey and C. Hardman, eds. *Paganism Today*. London: Thorsons, 1996.

MacLellan, G. *Shamanism*. London: Piatkus, 1999.

Macnulty, W. *Freemasonry*. London: Thames & Hudson, 1991.

Marwick, M., ed. *Witchcraft and Sorcery*. London: Penguin, 1990.

McKie, R. *ApeMan: the Story of Human Evolution*. London: BBC, 2000.

Morgan, L. H. *The league of the Iroquois*. In: M. Mead and R. Bunzel, eds. *The Golden Age of American Anthropology*. New York: George Braziller, 1960.

Pennick, N. *Practical Magic in the Northern Tradition*. Loughborough: Thoth, 1994.

Piggott, S. *The Druids*. London: Thames & Hudson, 1989.

Rasmussen, K. *A shaman's journey to the sea spirit*. In: W. Lessa and E. Vogt, eds. *Reader in Comparative Religion: an Anthropological Approach*. New York: Harper & Row, 1979.

Roper, L. *Oedipus and the Devil: Witchcraft, Sexuality and Religion in Early Modern Europe*. London: Routledge, 1994.

Rosen, B., ed. *Witchcraft*. London: Edward Arnold, 1969.

Shallcrass, P. *Druidry today*. In: G. Harvey and C. Hardman, eds. *Paganism Today*. London: Thorsons, 1996.

Sharpe, J. *Instruments of Darkness: Witchcraft in England 1550-1750*. London: Penguin, 1996.

Stanford, P. *The Devil: a Biography*. London: Mandarin, 1997.

Starhawk. *Dreaming the Dark*. Boston: Beacon, 1982.

Starhawk. *The Spiral Dance*. San Francisco: Harper & Row, 1989.

Stevens, A. *On Jung*. London: Penguin, 1991.

Sullivan, L. *Hidden Truths: Magic, Alchemy and the Occult*. New York: Macmillan, 1989.

Sun Bear, Wabun Wind and Crysalis Mulligan. *Dancing with the Wheel: the Medicine Wheel Workbook*. New York: Fireside Books, 1992.

Thomas, K. *Religion and the Decline of Magic*. London: Penguin, 1973.

Valiente, D. *Witchcraft for Tomorrow*. London: Robert Hale, 1985.

Warner, M. *Joan of Arc: the Image of Female Heroism*. London: Penguin, 1981.

Washington, P. *Madame Blavatsky's Baboon*. London: Secker & Warburg, 1993.

Wilson, C. *Witches*. Limpsfield: Dragon's World, 1989.

York, M. *The Emerging Network: a Sociology of the New Age and Neo-Pagan Movements*. Lanham, MD: Rowman & Littlefield, 1994.

## SUGGESTED SOURCES FOR FURTHER READING

Anthropological study of ritual in Africa:

Turner, V. *The Forest of Symbols: Aspects of Ndembu Ritual*. London: Cornell University Press, 1972.

Anthropological studies of spirit healing:

Kapferer, B. *A Celebration of Demons: Exorcism and Aesthetics of Healing in Sri Lanka*. 1991.

Katz, R. *The Straight Path of the Spirit: Ancestral Wisdom and Healing Traditions in Fiji*. Vermont: Park Street Press.

Anthropological study of sorcery:

Kapferer, B. *The Feast of the Sorcerer: Practices of Consciousness and Power*. Chicago: University of Chicago Press, 1997.

Western shamanism:

Larsen, S. *The Shaman's Doorway: Opening Imagination to Power and Myth*. Vermont: Inner Traditions International, 1998.

Noel, D. *The Soul of Shamanism: Western Fantasies, Imaginal Realities*. New York: Continuum, 1997.

History of Western Magic:

Snyder, C. *Exploring the World of King Arthur*. London: Thames & Hudson, 2000.

Yates, F. *Giordano Bruno & the Hermetic Tradition*. Chicago: University of Chicago Press, 1991.

Paganism:

Albanese, C. *Nature Religion in America*. Chicago: University of Chicago Press, 1991.

Billington, S. and Green, M., eds. *The Concept of the Goddess*. London: Routledge, 1999.

Greenwood, S. *Magic, Witchcraft and the Otherworld*. Oxford: Berg, 2000.

Hume, L. *Witchcraft and Paganism in Australia*. Melbourne: Melbourne University Press, 1997.

Sutcliffe, S. and Bowman, M., eds. *Beyond the New Age: Exploring Alternative Spirituality*. Edinburgh: Edinburgh University Press, 2000.

# PICTURE ACKNOWLEDGEMENTS

AKG: p10B Socrates and disciples. p11T Atlantis. p20T Hypnotic session, Sven Richard Bergh. p26B Knights of the Round Table. p29B Marching Infantry. p36T Pan. p38BR Artemis Ephesia, Erich Lessing. p39T Diana's Hunt, Luca Giordano. p40T Stag god Cerunnos, Erich Lessing. p80B Freyja. p81B Winter Solstice. Bridgeman Art Library: p8T Buddha. p8B The Annunciation, Italian School. p9M 'H' in the form of two conjurors. p9TR Alchemy master. p16T Friedrich Anton Mesmer, French School. p38BL Persephone, Anthony Frederick Augustus Sandys. p40B Pan and Psyche, Sir Edward Burne-Jones. p54T Diana, Agostino di Duccio. p64B Days of Creation, Sir Edward Burne-Jones. p64T Annunciation, Fra Angelico. p65B Angel, Sir Edward Burne-Jones. p66R Beguiling of Merlin, Sir Edward Burne-Jones. p66L Bedivere returns Excalibur to the lake, Roman du Saint Graal. p67T Last Supper, Francesco Bassano. p67B King Arthur, Lancelot and the Lady, Roman de Tristan. p68T Stonehenge, Italian School. p68B Wicker Man, Italian School. p75B Fairy Tree, Richard Doyle. p76BL Mandan Medicine Man, George Catlin. p77TL Pehriska-Ruhpa, Karl Bodmer (after). p80T Odin. p84B Sir Francis Dashwood, Bartolommeo Nazari. p85TL François Rabelais, Eugène Delacroix. p85TR Satan Arousing the Rebel Angels, William Blake. p90 Thanatos, Jacek Malczewski. Camera Press: p48BL Alex Sanders, John Drysdale. p49BL John Drysdale. p49TL. John Drysdale. p49TR John Hedgecoe. Christine Osborne Pictures: p36B Secret Wicca Ritual. p37T Sacred Goddess Altar. p47TL Goddess. p49BR Artefacts used in Wicca ceremonies. p57B Sacred rites: Goddess Festival, Glastonbury 2000. p58T Starhawk. p58B Sacred spiral dance. p59 'Black madonna'. p76T Drumming class. p77TR Dream rings. CORBIS: p42B Raymond Gehman. p74T People dancing in the Findhorn Foundation, Sandro Vannini. p75T Musicians of the Paul Winter Consort, Roger Ressmeyer. p85B La Vey conducts a devilish service, Bettmann. p87B Charles Manson, Bettmann. e.t.archive: p9TM Nostradamus. p10T Mosaic of Triumph of Poseidon and his wife. p15T Candidate for Master, Freemasonry. p15B Frontispiece to History of Freemasonry. p24B Tarot card: the King of Wands, Frieda Harris. p29T Inside the Temple of the Grail, W. Hauschild. p54B Diana Bathing, François Boucher. p82BR Casket with runic inscriptions. Fortean Picture Library: p12M Tarot cards from the Waite pack. p12BL Eliphas Levi. p17TL Madame Blavatsky. p19R Samuel Liddell MacGregor Mathers. p25TR Blood on the Moon, Austin Osman Spare. p25TL Resurrection of Zoroaster, Austin Osman Spare. p32B White witchcraft altar, Kevin Carlyon. p34T Gerald Gardner, Raymond Buckland. p37BL Drawing down the moon. p42T Winter Solstice ritual, Kevin Carlyon. p43TM Kevin Carlyon binding new initiates, Kevin Carlyon. p47B Wiccan initiation, Raymond Buckland. p50T Raymond Buckland. p50B Priest enters the Temple, Raymond Buckland. p51T Samhain ceremony, Raymond Buckland. p51B Wiccan High Priest and High Priestess, Raymond Buckland. p53BR Title page of Leland's Aradia. p53T Cornish witches invoking the 'owlman', Anthony Shiels. p55T Cornish witch Cait Sidh. p55B Witches dancing at midnight. p69B Emma Restall-Orr, Kevin Carlyon. p71T Arch-Druid at Avebury, Summer Solstice, Clive Odinson. p71B Druids at Winter Solstice, Stonehenge, Clive Odinson. p72BL Celtic music at Roughtor, Paul Broadhurst. p72BR Edgar Cayce Foundation, Klaus Aarsleff. p73T Fountain International members, Paul Broadhurst. p73B Tourist doing Tai Chi, Klaus Aarsleff. p74BL Eileen Caddy, Dr Elmar R Gruber. p74BR Findhorn meditation room, Tony Healy. p78B Man meditating at Medicine Wheel, Arizona, Klaus Aarsleff. p83TL Rune stones, Klaus Aarsleff. Susan Greenwood: p41(all) owl mask, plaque and Baubo made by Maria Strutz. p79TR Jo Crow. p91(all) Baphomet, Chaos mask, Chaos Tantric altar. Hulton Picture Library: p12TR A. E. Waite. p16BL Helena Petrovna Blavatsky. p16BR Henry Steel Olcott. p17TR Annie Besant. p17B Krishnamurti with Annie Besant. p18BR Miss Annie Horniman. p21TR Garb of the Golden Dawn, Aleister Crowley. p21BL Alan Bennett. p22BM Aleister Crowley in robes of Golden Dawn. p22TR Aleister Crowley. p23BL Self-portrait – Aleister Crowley. p23TR Certificate acknowledging Crowley as member of High Order of Freemasons. p24T Aleister Crowley, Fosco Maraini. p35B Margaret Murray. p56T Jules Michelet. p86B Jayne Mansfield, Keystone Press Agency. p88BR Sex Pistols. p88BL Austin Osman Spare, Bert Hardy. Hutchison Library: p11ML Ya-uli. p11BR Atlantean Mystery Pyramid. p13B Tree of Life. p13TR Cabbala, Great Countenance. p14T Rosicrucian – reincarnation. p14B Rosicrucian Rosy Cross. p20BL Order of Pectoral. p20BM Pectoral Cross. p20BR Symbol used in Hermes Lodge of Stella Matutina. p53T Drawing down the moon. p77B Shamanistic drum. p84T Devils pact. p86T Anton La Vey. p87TR Woman devil. James Wood: p79BR Modern Western shaman. Mark Fiennes: p38 Diana, Frans Floris. Mary Evans Picture Library: p18T William Butler Yeats. p18B Maud Gonne. p25B Symbolic painting for Crowley's Temple of the A.A, JFC Fulle p27B Carl Gustav Jung. p27T The Passing of Arthur. p56B Witchcraft in flight. p57 Susan B Anthony. p70T Druid priestess. p70B Druids of Anglesey. p87TL Ceremoni seal designed by Aleister Crowley. Mick Sharp Photography: p32T Modern offering left beside prehistoric rock carvings. p33T Tintagel Castle, Cornwall. p33B Madro Well. p45T Bethesda Woods. p72T Sunset from Snowdon summit. Peter Newark Pictures: p21BR Samuel Mathers and Mina Mathers. Rex Features: p30. p35T Wick Man, Lesley Smith. p73TR James Lovelock. p82T May Day, Northern Ireland, Lesle Smith. Sally Griffyn: p46T Doreen Valiente. p63B Using a crystal ball. Society of th Inner Light: p26T Dion Fortune. p28B Dion Fortune. Tony Stone Images: p44T Wat droplet on pink heather, Charles Krebs. Werner Forman Archive: p44–45B Ring Brodgar. p81T Detail of 12th-century Viking tapestry.

# TEXT NOTES

These references give the sources for direct and indirect quotes within the text.

p 11 Luce, J. *The End of Atlantis*. London: BCA, 1973.

p 13 Wang, R. *The Qabalistic Tarot*. York Beach, Maine: Samuel Weiser, 1983.

p 14 King, F. *Modern Ritual Magic*. Bridport, Dorset: Prism, 1990.

p 24 Crowley, A. *Magick in Theory and Practice*. Secaucus, NJ: Castle 1991.

p 29 Fortune, D. *The Sea Priestess*. Wellingborough: Aquarian, 1989.

p 36 Gardner, G. *Witchcraft Today*. New York: Magickal Childe, 198

p 40 Gadon, E. *The Once and Future Goddess*. Wellingborough: Aquarian, 1990.

p 47 Kelly, A. *Crafting the Art of Magic: a History of Modern Witchcraft 1939–1964*. St Paul, MN: Llewellyn, 1991.

p 51 Buckland, R. *The Complete Book of Saxon Witchcraft*. York Beach Maine: Samuel Weiser, 1989.

p 82 Willis, T. *Discover Runes*. London: Harper Collins, 1986.

p 83 Pennick, N. *Practical Magic in the Northern Tradition*. Loughborough: Thoth, 1994.

p 86 La Vey, A. *The Satanic Bible*. New York: Avon Books, 1969.

p 90 Hine, P. *Condensed Chaos*. Arizona: New Falcon Publications, 1995.

p 90 Carroll, P. *Liber Null and Psychonaut*. York Beach, ME: Samuel Weiser, 1987.

# INDEX

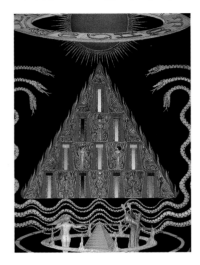